Fife Stree

CONTEN

Area of Coverage	2 - 3	Kenn	
Aberdour, Auchtertool, Auchtermuchty & indices	4 - 5	Kettle	
Anstruther, Kilrenny & index	6 - 7	Petty	
Auchterderran, Cardenden & index	8 - 9	Kincar... ...index	64 - 65
Ballingry, Crosshill, Lochore & index	10 - 11	Kirkcaldy	66 - 71
Balmullo, Blairhall, Cairneyhill, Dairsie & indices	12 - 13	Ladybank, Leuchars & indices	72 - 73
Burntisland & index	14 - 15	Leven & Innerleven	74 - 75
Carnock, Gowkhall, Oakley & index	16 - 17	Lochgelly & index	76 - 77
Ceres, Crail & indices	18 - 19	Lower Largo & index	78 - 79
Charlestown & Limekilns	20 - 21	Methil & Buckhaven	80 - 81
Coaltown of, East & West Wemyss & index	22 - 23	Newburgh, Pitlessie & indices	82 - 83
Cowdenbeath & Lumphinnans	24 - 25	Pittenweem, St Monans & index	84 - 85
Crossford, Crossgates & indices	26 - 27	St Andrews	86 - 87
Culross, Valleyfield & index	28 - 29	Saline, Springfield, Strathkinness & indices	88 - 89
Cupar	30 - 31	Strathmiglo, Torryburn & indices	90 - 91
Dalgety Bay & index	32 - 33	Tayport & index	92 - 93
Dunfermline & index	34 - 41	Thornton, Windygates & indices	94 - 95
Earlsferry, Elie, Falkland & indices	42 - 43	Wormit, Newport-on-Tay	96 - 97
Freuchie, Gauldry, Guardbridge & indices	44 - 45	Index section:	98 - 110
Glenrothes	46 - 53	Cowdenbeath, Cupar, Glenrothes,	
Inverkeithing, Rosyth & North Queensferry	54 - 57	Inverkeithing, Kirkcaldy, Leven, St Andrews,	
Kelty, Kingsbarns, Kingseat & indices	58 - 59	Wormit & Newport-on-Tay	

KEY TO MAP SYMBOLS

M90	Motorway	S F		Superstore / filling station
A92	Primary route dual / single	PO L		Post office / library
A921	A road dual / single	m a		Museum / antiquity
B917	B road dual / single	⚔ ✕		Castle / battlefield
	Unclassified road	🏠 ✳		Historic house / garden
	Pedestrianised road	△ ⊕		Camping / caravan site
	Track / path	i ✸		Tourist information / other tourist attraction
	Long distance path	✝		Church or place of worship
	Railway & station			Woodland
	Disused railway or tunnel			Park / cemetery / sports or recreation
✈ B	Airport / bus station			Built up area
▲ ▼ △	Primary / secondary / special or private school			Rocks
◆ ◆ ◆	Police / fire / ambulance station			Sand
◆ ◇	Lifeboat / coastguard station			Shingle
P H	Parking / hospital			Mud

Scale 1:14 000

0 — 500m
0 — 500yds

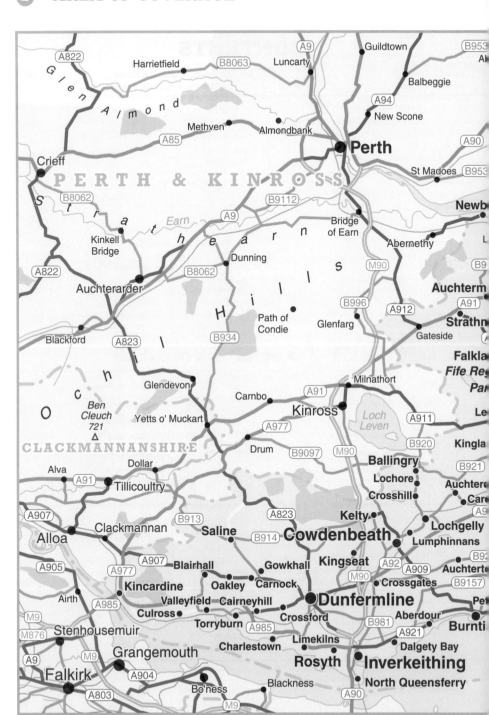

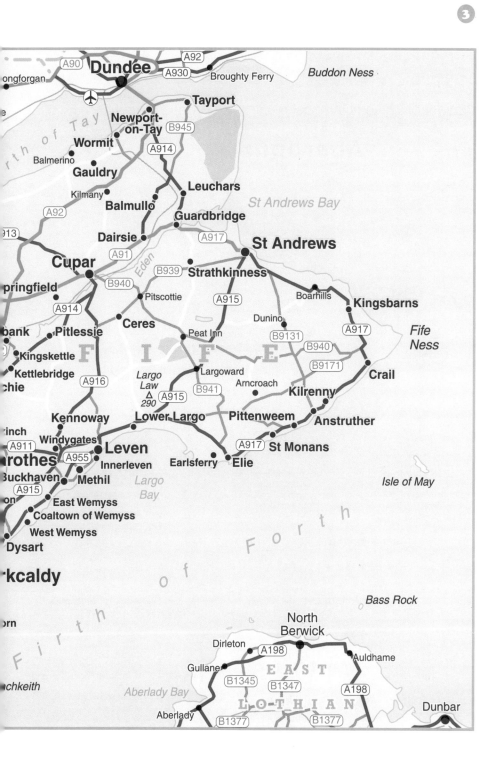

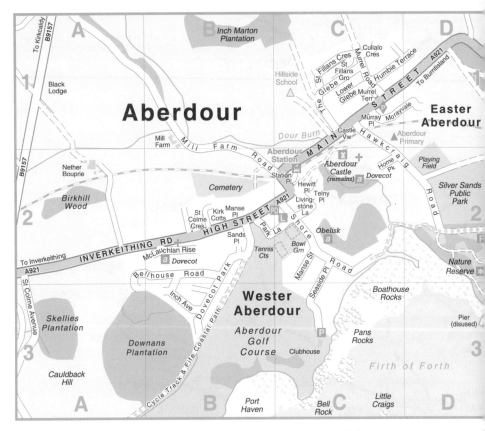

Index to Aberdour

Bellhouse Road	B2
Castle View	C1
Cullalo Crescent	C1
Dovecot Park	B3
Glebe, The	C1
Hawkcraig Road	C1
Hewitt Place	C2
High Street	B2
Home Park	C2
Humbie Terrace	C1
Inch Avenue	B3
Inverkeithing Road	A2
Kirk Cottages	B2
Livingstone Lane	C2
Lower Glebe	C1
McLauchlan Rise	B2
Main Street	C1
Manse Place	B2
Manse Street	C2
Mill Farm Road	B1
Morayvale	C1
Murray Place	C1
Murrel Road	C1
Murrel Terrace	C1
Park Lane	B2
St Colme Avenue	C2
St Colme Crescent	C1
St Fillans Crescent	C1
St Fillans Grove	C1
Sands Place	B2
Seaside Place	C2
Shore Road	C1
Station Place	C1
Telny Place	C1

Index to Auchtertool

Camilla Grove
Camilla Road
Clifton Cottages
Garden Cottages
Halyard Terrace
Main Street
Maltings, The
Milton Bank
Milton Park
Moray Court
Newbigging Terrace
Newbigging
Sanderson Terrace

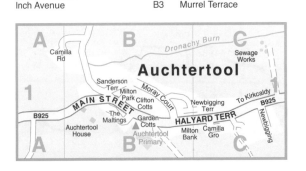

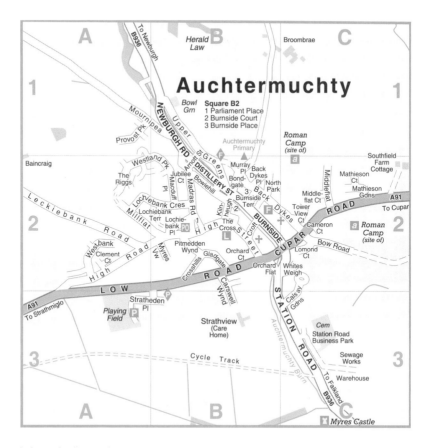

Auchtermuchty

Square B2
1 Parliament Place
2 Burnside Court
3 Burnside Place

Index to Auchtermuchty

Arnott Street	B1	High Road	A2	Newburgh Road	B1
Back Dykes Place	B2	High Street	B2	North Park	B2
Back Dykes	B2	Jubilee Court	B2	Orchard Court	B2
Bondgate	B2	Kilnheugh	B2	Orchard Flat	B2
Bow Road	C2	Lochiebank Crescent	A2	Parliament Place (1)	B2
Bowiehill	B2	Lochiebank Place	B2	Pitmedden Wynd	B2
Burnside	B2	Lochiebank Terrace	B2	Provost Park	A1
Burnside Court (2)	B2	Leckiebank Road	A2	Riggs, The	A2
Burnside Place (3)	B2	Lomond Court	C2	Station Road	C3
Burnside Terrace	B2	Low Road	B2	Stratheden Place	A3
Calsay Gardens	C3	MacDuff Place	B2	Tower View Court	C2
Cameron Court	C2	Madras Road	B2	Upper Greens	B1
Carswell Wynd	B2	Mathieson Court	C2	Westbank	A2
Clement Court	A2	Mathieson Gardens	C2	Westland Park	A2
Croft	B2	Middleflat Court	C2	Whites Weigh	C2
Cross, The	B2	Middleflat	C2		
Crosshills	B2	Millflat	A2		
Cupar Road	C2	Mournipea	A1		
Distillery Street	B2	Murray Place	B2		
Gladgate	B2	Myres View	B2		

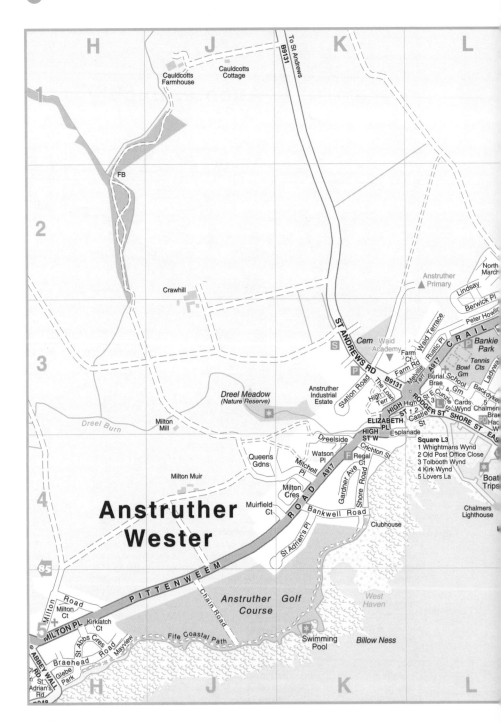

H J K L

To St Andrews
B9131

Cauldcotts
Farmhouse
Cauldcotts
Cottage

1

FB

2

North
March

Anstruther
Primary

Lindsay

Crawhill

Berwick Pl

Peter Howlin

CRAIL

Cem Waid
Academy

Rustic Pl

P Bankie
Park

Wald Terrace

Farm
Ct

Tennis
Cts

Ladywa

3

Melville Terr

Farm Rd

Bowl
Grn

School

Burial
Brae

Backdyke

P

Dreel Meadow
(Nature Reserve)

Anstruther
Industrial
Estate

St Andrews Rd

B9131

The Loan

Station Road

High
Terr

High High
ST 1 2

Cunzie St

Cards
Wynd

4. Grn

3

Chalmers

5

Shore St Eas

Rodger St

Castle
St

Hac
W

Dreel Burn

Milton
Mill

ELIZABETH
PL

Esplanade

HIGH
ST W

Square L3
1 Whightmans Wynd
2 Old Post Office Close
3 Tolbooth Wynd
4 Kirk Wynd
5 Lovers La

Dreelside

Dreelside

HIGH

Crichton St

Queens
Gdns

Watson
Pl

Regal
Ct

A917

Milton Muir

Mitchell
Pl

Gardner Ave

Shore Road

Boat
Trips

Chalmers
Lighthouse

Milton
Cres

Muirfield
Ct

Road

Bankwell Road

Clubhouse

4

**Anstruther
Wester**

St Adrians Pl

85

PITTENWEEM

Chain Road

West
Haven

**Anstruther Golf
Course**

Road
Milton
Ct

Milton

MILTON PL

Kirklatch
Ct

Fife Coastal Path

Swimming
Pool

Billow Ness

St Abbs Cres

Road

Mayview

Braehead

Glebe
Park

ABBEY WALL

St
Adrian's
Rd

H J K L

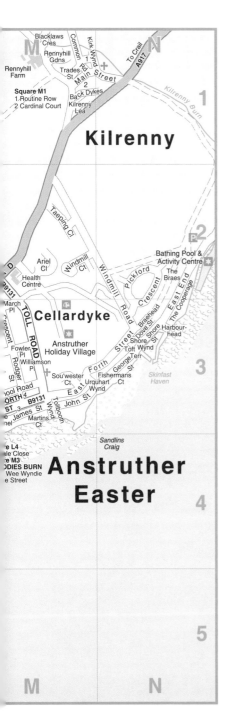

Index to Anstruther

Abbey Wall Road	H5	Main Street	M1
Ariel Close	M2	March Crescent	M3
Back Dykes	M1	March Place	M3
Backdykes	L3	March Road	L2
Bankwell Road	K4	Martins Court	M3
Blacklaws Crescent	M1	Mayview Avenue	L3
Blyth Court	M3	Mayview Court	L3
Braehead	N3	Mayview Road	L3
Braehead Road	H5	Mayview	H5
Braes, The	N2	Melville Terrace	L3
Burial Brae	L3	Milton Court	H5
Burnside Place	M3	Milton Crescent	K4
Burnside Terrace	M3	Milton Place	H5
Caddies Burn (2)	M3	Milton Road	H5
Cardinal Court (2)	M1	Mitchell Place	K4
Cards Wynd	L3	Muirfield Court	J4
Castle Street	L3	Murray Square	M3
Chain Road	J5	North March	L2
Chalmers Brae	L3	Old Post Office Close (2)	L3
Common Road	M1	Peter Howling Place	L3
Cooperage, The	N3	Pickford Crescent	N2
Crail Road	L3	Pittenweem Road	J5
Crichton Street	K4	Priory Court	H5
Cunzie Street	L3	Queens Gardens	J4
Dove Street	N3	Regal Court	K4
Dreelside	K4	Rennyhill Gardens	M1
East End	N3	Rodger Street (Anstruther)	L3
East Forth Street	M3	Rodger Street (Cellardyke)	M3
East Green	L3	Routine Row (1)	M1
East Shore	L3	Rustic Place	L3
Elizabeth Place	K3	St Abbs Crescent	H5
Ellice Street (4)	M3	St Adrian's Place	K5
Esplanade	K3	St Adrian's Road	H5
Farm Court	L3	St Andrews Road	K3
Farm Road	K3	St Ayles Crescent	L3
Fishermans Court	N3	School Green	L3
Fowler Place	M3	School Road	M3
Fowler Street	M3	Shore Road	K4
Gardner Avenue	K4	Shore Street (Anstruther)	L3
George Street	N3	Shore Street (Cellardyke)	N3
Glebe Park	H5	Shore Wynd	N3
Glenburn Road	M3	Sou'wester Court	M3
Glenogil Gardens	L3	Station Road	K3
Haddfoot Wynd	L3	Taeping Close	M2
Harbour View	L3	Toft Terrace	N3
Harbourhead	N3	Tolbooth Wynd (3)	L3
Harbourlea	L3	Toll Road	M3
High Street	K3	Tollbooth Wynd	M3
High Street East	L3	Trades Street	M1
High Street West	K4	Union Place	L3
High Terrace	K3	Urquhart Wynd	N3
James Street	M3	Vennel, The	M3
John Street	M3	Waggon Road	H5
Kilrenny Lea	M1	Waid Terrace	L3
Kirk Wynd (4)	L3	Watson Place	K4
(Anstruther)		Wee Wyndie, The (3)	M3
Kirk Wynd (Kilrenny)	M1	West Forth Street	M3
Kirklatch Court	H5	Whale Close (1)	L4
Ladywalk	L3	Whightmans Wynd (1)	L3
Lindsay Berwick Place	L2	Williamson Place	M3
Loan, The	K3	Windmill Court	M2
Lovers Lane (5)	L3	Windmill Road	N2

A B C D

1
Woodend
Park

KINGLASSIE B921 RD
To Kinglassie
Works

Woodend
Balgreggie
Farm

WOODEND ROAD

2
Auchterderran
Golf
Course

Clubhouse
Playing
Field
Balgreggie Pk
Balgreggie Pk Road
Craigside Road

Auchterderran

Playing
Fields
Playing
Field
Kirk Burn

Res

War
Meml
Woodside Terr
Balderran Dr
Murray-
knowe
Silverton Dr

Kirk Burn
Daisyfield
Terr
West-
field
Brae
Craig Road
Silverton Dr
Derran Drive
St Ninian's
RC Primary

3
Jamphlars
Golf View
JAMPHLARS ROAD
B921
MAIN STREET
Thomson Ct
Cem
Kirkburn Drive
Westfield Terr
Kinshotts Terr
Kinshotts Drive

To Lochgelly
B981
Bowhill View
Jamphlars Pl
Jamphlars Ct
Wallsgreen Gdns
Derran Road
Church Pl
Orebank Road
Bowhill
Parsons
Mill

Jamphlars Pl
Wallsgreen Rd
PO P
Swimming
Pool
L
Station Rd
Bowl Gm
Bowhill
Bridge
Gammie
Pl
River Ore

4
Wallsgreen Park
Recreation Ground
STATION ROAD
CARDENDEN ROAD
Cardenden Road
PO P

Denend
Primary
School La
Station Road
Den Ct
Main Road
Hyndloup Terr
Carden Castle Park
Carden Castle Park
Carden
Castle
Pk

Cardenden
Station
FB
P
Ian
Rankin
Ct
Carden Castle
Carden Castle

5
Denfield Gdns
Denfield Drive
Denfield Avenue
Denfield
Denend
Cotts
Cardenden
Primary
Carden Avenue
Playing
Field
Carde

Dundonald
Bluebell Gardens
Dundonald Park
Dundonald Crescent
Den Burn

6
Spittal
Spittal Den
Wood
Glen
Lodge
Moorside
Park
(Football
Grd)
Dundonald Pk
Dundonald
Park
Road
Cardenba

A B C D

Index to Auchterderran & Cardenden

Balderran Drive	C3	Wallsgreen Road	B3
Balgreggie Park	B2	Westfield Brae	C3
Balgreggie Road	C2	Westfield Terrace	C3
Bluebell Gardens	C5	Whitehall Avenue	E4
Bowhill View	A3	Whitehall Crescent	E4
Bowhouse Terrace	E4	Whitehall Drive	E5
Carden Avenue	D4, D5	Woodend Park	A2
Carden Castle Avenue	D5	Woodend Road	B2
Carden Castle Park	D5	Woodside Terrace	C3
Carden Crescent	D4		
Cardenbarns Road	D6		
Cardenden Road	C4		
Church Place	C3		
Cluny Park	D4		
Cluny Square	F4		
Craigmead Terrace	C3		
Craigside Road	C2		
Daisyfield Terrace	C3		
Den Court	C4		
Denend Cottages	C5		
Denfield Avenue	C5		
Denfield Drive	C5		
Denfield Gardens	C5		
Derran Drive	C3		
Dundonald Crescent	C5		
Dundonald Park	C5, C6		
Forest Road	D4		
Gammie Place	C4		
Golf View	A3		
Hyndloup Terrace	D4		
Ian Rankin Court	C5		
Jamphlars Court	B3		
Jamphlars Place	B3		
Jamphlars Road	B3		
Keirs Brae	E5		
Kinglassie Road	B1		
Kirkburn Drive	C3		
Kirkshotts Terrace	C3		
Main Road	C5		
Main Street	B3		
Muirtonhill Road	A2		
Murrayknowe	C3		
Orebank Road	C3		
School Lane	C4		
Silverton Drive	C3		
Station Road	C4		
Sunnyside Road	E4		
Thomson Court	B3		
Wallsgreen Gardens	B3		

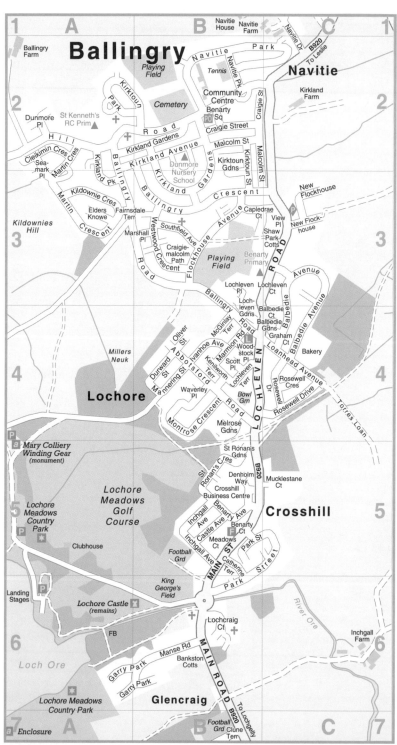

Ballingry

Navitie

Lochore

Crosshill

Glencraig

Ballingry Farm
Navitie House
Navitie Farm
Navitie Dr
B920
To Leslie

Navitie Park
Playing Field
Tennis
Community Centre
Kirkland Farm

Dunmore Pl
St Kenneth's RC Prim
Cemetery
Benarty Sq
Craigie Street

Cleikimin Cres
Kirktoun Park
Hill Road
Kirkland Gardens
Kirkland Avenue
Malcolm St
Kirktoun Gdns

Sea-mark Pl
Martin Cres
Ballingry Pk
Kirkland Pk
Dunmore Nursery School
Kirktoun St
Malcolm St

Martin Crescent
Kildownie Cres
Kirkland Gardens
Ballingry Crescent
New Flockhouse

Kildownies Hill
Elders Knowe
Fairnsdale Terr
Southfield Ave
Capledrae Ct
View Pl
Shaw Park Cotts
New Flockhouse

Marshall Pl
Westwood Crescent
Flockhouse
Craigie-malcolm Path
Ballingry Avenue
Benarty Primary
Road

Road
Ballingry Road
Playing Field
Avenue

Millers Neuk
Oliver St
McGinlay Terr
Lochleven Pl
Lochleven Ct
Balbedie Ct
Balbedie Gdns
Graham Ct
Balbedie Avenue
Bakery

Lochore
Abbotsford
Ivanhoe Ave
Lochleven Gdns
Marmion Rd
Woodstock Pl
Scott Pl
Balbedie Gdns
Loanhead Avenue

Durward St
Mannering St
Kenilworth Terr
Lochleven Terr
Lochleven Dr
Rosewell Cres

Waverley Pl
Bowl Grn
Rosewell
Rosewell Drive
Torres Loan

Montrose Crescent
Road
Melrose Gdns

Mary Colliery Winding Gear (monument)
St Ronan's Gdns
St Ronan's Cres
Mucklestane Ct

Lochore Meadows Country Park
Lochore Meadows Golf Course
Denholm Way
Crosshill Business Centre
B920

Lochore Meadows Country Park
Clubhouse
Inchgall Ave
Benarty Ave
Castle Ave
Benarty Ct
Meadows Ct
Park St

Football Grd
Inchgall Ave
MAIN ST
Catherine Terr
Park Street

Landing Stages
King George's Field
Park

Lochore Castle (remains)
Lochcraig Ct
River Ore
Inchgall Farm

FB
Manse Rd
Bankston Cotts
MAIN ROAD

Loch Ore
Garry Park
Garry Park
To Lochgelly
B920

Lochore Meadows Country Park
Football Grd
Clune Terr

Enclosure

Index to Ballingry

Abbotsford Road	B4	Mannering Street	B4
Balbedie Avenue	C4	Manse Road	B6
Balbedie Court	C3	Marmion Road	B4
Balbedie Gardens	C4	Marshall Place	B3
Ballingry Crescent	B3	Martin Crescent	A3
Ballingry Road	A2, B3	Meadows Court	B5
Bankston Cottages	B6	Melrose Gardens	B4
Benarty Avenue	B5	Montrose Crescent	B4
Benarty Court	B5	Navitie Drive	C1
Benarty Square	B2	Navitie Park	B2
Capledrae Court	B3	New Flockhouse	C3
Castle Avenue	B5	Oliver Street	B4
Catherine Terrace	B5	Park Street	B5
Cleikimin Crescent	A2	Rosewell Crescent	C4
Clune Terrace	B7	Rosewell Drive	C4
Craigie Street	B2	St Ronan's Crescent	B5
Craigiemalcolm Path	B3	St Ronan's Gardens	B5
Denholm Way	B5	Scott Place	B4
Dunmore Place	A2	Seamark Place	A2
Durward Street	B4	Shaw Park Cottages	C3
Elders Knowe	A3	Southfield Avenue	B3
Fairnsdale Terrace	A3	Torres Loan	C4
Flockhouse Avenue	B3	View Place	C3
Garry Park	A6	Waverley Place	B4
Graham Court	C4	Westwood Crescent	B3
Hill Road	A2	Woodstock Place	B4
Inchgall Avenue	B5		
Ivanhoe Avenue	B4		
Kenilworth Terrace	B4		
Kildownie Crescent	A3		
Kirkland Avenue	B2		
Kirkland Gardens	A2		
Kirkland Park	A2		
Kirktoun Gardens	B2		
Kirktoun Park	A2		
Kirktoun Street	B2		
Loanhead Avenue	C4		
Lochcraig Court	B6		
Lochleven Court	C3		
Lochleven Gardens	B3		
Lochleven Place	B3		
Lochleven Road	B4		
Lochleven Terrace	B4		
McGinlay Terrace	B4		
Main Road	B6		
Main Street	B5		
Malcolm Street	B2		

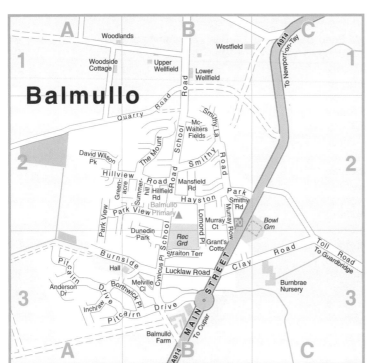

Index to Balmullo

Anderson Drive	A
Borthwick Place	A
Burnside	A
Clay Road	B
Cynicus Place	B
David Wilson Park	A
Dunedin Park	B
Grant's Cottages	B
Greenacre	A
Hayston Park	B
Hillfield Road	B
Hillview Road	A
Inchlaw	A
Lomond Place	B
Lucklaw Road	B
McWalters Fields	B
Main Street	B
Mansfield Road	B
Melville Close	B
Mount, The	B
Murray Court	B
Murray Row	B
Park View	A
Pitcairn Drive	A
Quarry Road	B
School Road	B2, B
Smithy Lane	B
Smithy Road	B
Straiton Terrace	B
Summerhill	B
Toll Road	C

Index to Blairhall

Blair Grove	A1
Bowling Green Wynd	A2
Clover Way	A1
East Avenue	A2
Houldsworth Street	A2
Overton Farm Cottages	A1
Rintoul Avenue	A1
Rintoul Place	A1
School Lane	A1
South Avenue	A2
Wemyss Avenue	A1
Wilson Street	A1
Woodlands Terrace	B1

Index to Dairsie

Ardencaple Terrace	A2
Edenbank Cottages	B2
Main Street	A2
Orchard Park	A2
Osnaburgh Court	A2
Station Road	B2
Vantage Cottages	A2
Woodville Park	A2

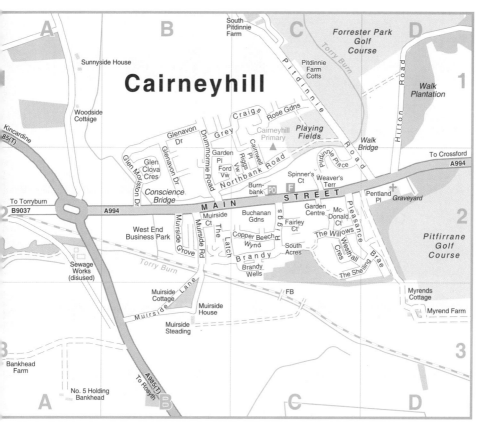

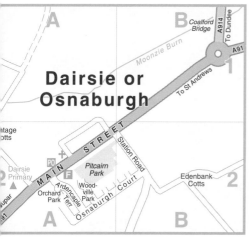

Index to Cairneyhill

Brandy Riggs	C2	Main Street	C2
Brandy Wells	C2	Muirside Court	B2
Buchanan Gardens	C2	Muirside Grove	B2
Burnbank	C2	Muirside Lane	B3
Cairnwell Place	C2	Muirside Road	B2
Copper Beech	C2	Northbank Road	C2
Wynd		Pentland Place	D2
Drummormie Road	B1	Pitdinnie Farm	C1
Fairley Court	C2	Cottages	
Ford View	B2	Pitdinnie Place	C2
Garden Place	B2	Pitdinnie Road	C1
Glen Clova	B2	Pleasance Brae	C2
Crescent		Riggs View	C2
Glen Moriston	B2	Rose Gardens	C1
Drive		Sheiling, The	D2
Glenavon Drive	B1	South Acres	C2
Grey Craigs	B1	Spinner's Court	C2
Hilton Road	D1, D2	Weaver's Terrace	C2
Latch, The	B2	Westhall Crescent	C2
McDonald Court	C2	Willows, The	C2

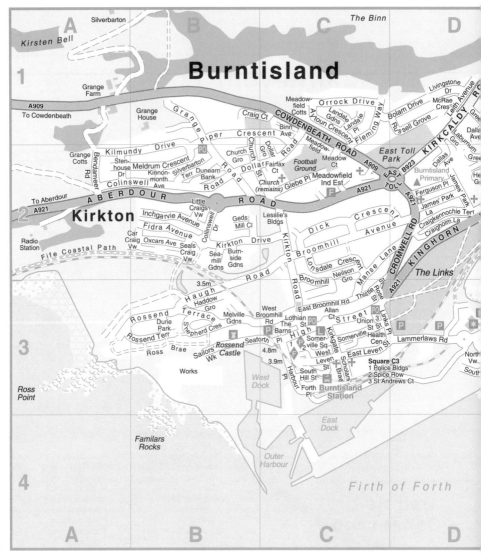

Index to Burntisland

		Car Craig View	B2	Dick Crescent	C
		Church Street	B1	Dollar Grove	C
Aberdour Road	A2	Church Grove	B2	Dollar Road	B
Allan Court	C3	Colinswell Road	A2	Duncanson Drive	E
Aytoun Crescent	C1	Collinswell Drive	B2	Dunearn Bank	B
Barns, The	C3	Cotburn Crescent	D1	Durie Park	B
Bendameer Road	A2	Cowdenbeath Road	C1	East Broomhill Road	C
Binn Avenue	C1	Craig Court	B1	East Leven Street	C
Bolam Drive	D1	Craigholm Lane	D2	East Toll	C
Broomhill	C3	Craigkennochie Terrace	D2	Fairfax Court	C
Broomhill Avenue	C2	Cromwell Road	D2	Ferguson Place	D
Burnside Gardens	B2	Dallas Avenue	D2	Fidra Avenue	B

E F

Dodhead
Golf
Course

High Bents

1

y Crescent MacDonald Pl

uncanson Drive   Cemetery Linwell Ct   To Kirkcaldy
                                          A921
KINGHORN   ROAD

Fife Coastal Path

2

er

3

Black
Rocks

oy

4

E F

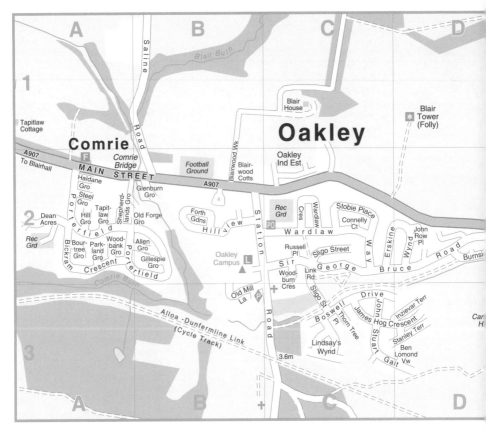

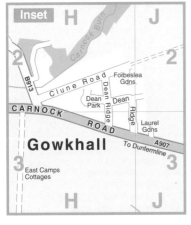

Index to Carnock, Gowkhall & Oakley

Allen Grove	B2	Carnock Mill	
Ash Grove	F3	Carnock Road	G2
Ben Lomond View	D3	Clune Road	
Bickram Crescent	A2	Connelly Court	
Blairwood Cottages	B2	Croft Gardens	
Blairwood Walk	B2	Dean Acres	
Bonhard Road	E2	Dean Park	
Boswell Drive	C3	Dean Ridge	
Bourtree Grove	A2	East Camps Cottages	
Burnbank	F2	Erskine Wynd	
Burnside Terrace	D2	Forbeslea Gardens	
Camps Road	F3	Forth Gardens	
Carneil Road	F3	Gillespie Grove	
Carneil Terrace	F3	Glenburn Grove	

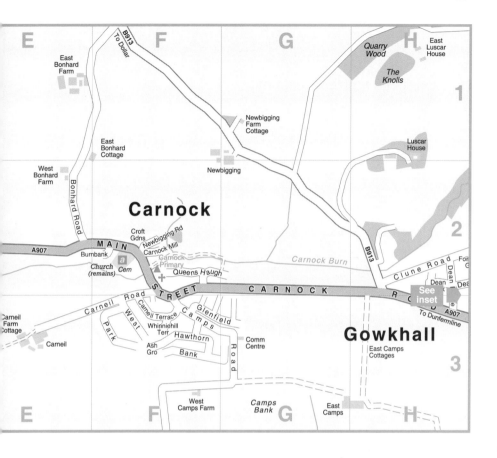

field	F3	Newbigging Road	F2	Stobie Place	C2
ane Grove	A2	Old Forge Grove	A2	Tapitlaw Grove	A2
thorn Bank	F3	Old Mill Lane	B3	Thorn Tree Place	C3
Grove	A2	Parkland Grove	A2	Wardlaw Crescent	C2
ew	B2	Porterfield	A2	Wardlaw Way	C2
var Terrace	D3	Queens Haugh	F2	West Park	F3
es Hog Crescent	C3	Russell Place	C2	Whinniehill Terrace	F3
Row Place	D2	Saline Road	B1	Woodbank Grove	A2
Stuart Gait	C3	Shepherdlands Grove	A2	Woodburn Crescent	C2
say's Wynd	C3	Sir George Bruce Road	C2		
Road	C2	Sligo Street	C2, C3		
el Gardens	J3	Stanley Terrace	D3		
Street (Carnock)	F2	Station Road	B2		
Street (Oakley)	A2	Steel Grove	A2		

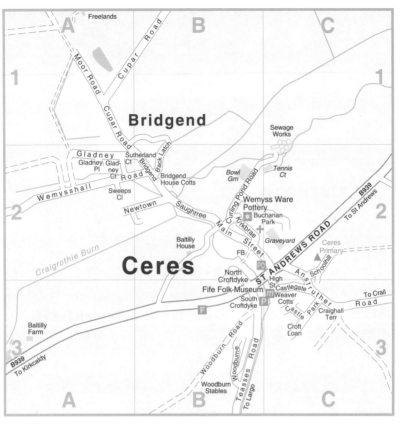

Index to Ceres

Anstruther Road	C3
Back Latch	B2
Bridgend	B2
Bridgend House Cottages	B2
Buchanan Park	B2
Castle Park	C3
Castlegate	C3
Craighall Terrace	C3
Croft Loan	C3
Cupar Road	A1
Curling Pond Road	B2
Gladney	A2
Gladney Court	A2
Gladney Place	A2
High Street	C3
Kirkbrae	B2
Main Street	B2
Moor Road	A1
Newtown	B2
North Croftdyke	B2
St Andrews Road	C2
Saughtree	B2
Schoolhill	C2
South Croftdyke	B3
Sutherland Court	A2
Sweeps Close	A2
Teasses Road	B3
Weaver Cottages	C3
Wemysshall Road	A2
Woodburn Road	B3
Woodburne	B3

Index to Crail

Albany Court (5)	B2
Anchorage, The (11)	B3
Anstruther Road	A3
Arrighi Crescent	B2
Auldwell Gardens	B2
Back Dykes	B2
Balcomie Green	C1
Balcomie Road	C1
Beech Walk	B2
Bow Butts	B2
Bow Butts Road	C2
Bowling Green Close (3)	B3
Bowling Green Place	A2
Brandy's Holme	B3
Butcher's Close (2)	B3
Calder Court	C3
Carr Crescent	A2
Castle Street	B3
Castle Terrace	B3
Castle Walk	
Collingwood Court (6)	
Cottage Row	
Denburn Place	
Dorward Drive	
Farm Cottages	A2,
Felkington Avenue	
Gifford Court	
Glebe, The	B2
High Street North	B2
High Street South	B2
King Street	
Kirk Wynd	
Kirkmay Road	
Lairsgate Road	B1

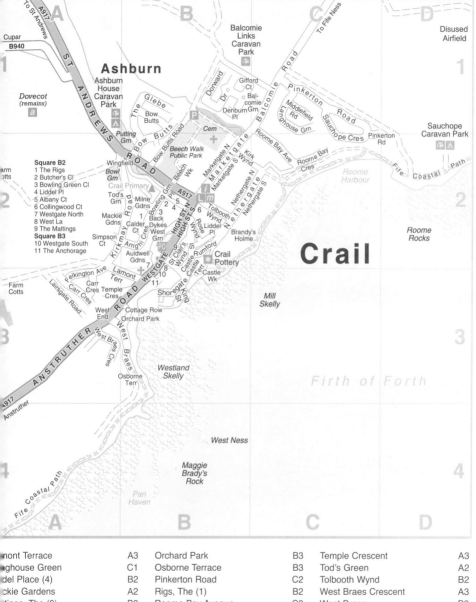

Crail

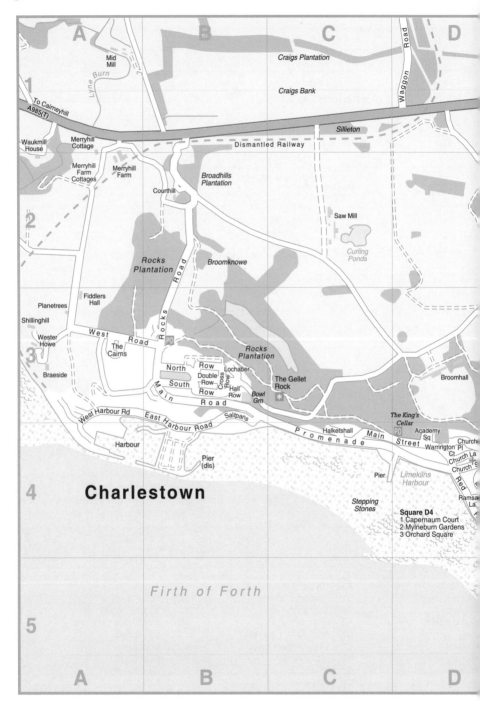

A985(T)
To Cairneyhill

Mid Mill

Lyne Burn

Craigs Plantation

Craigs Bank

Waggon Road

Sillieton

Waukmill House

Merryhill Cottage

Dismantled Railway

Merryhill Farm Cottages

Merryhill Farm

Courthill

Broadhills Plantation

Saw Mill

Rocks Plantation

Broomknowe

Curling Ponds

Fiddlers Hall

Planetrees

Shillinghill

Wester Howe

West Road

The Cairns

North Row

Double Row

South Row

Cross Row

Lochaber

Hall Row

Rocks Plantation

The Gellet Rock

Broomhall

Braeside

Main Road

Bowl Grn

Rocks Road

PO

West Harbour Rd

East Harbour Road

Saltpans

Halketshall

Promenade

Main Street

The King's Cellar

PO

Academy Sq

Warrington Pl

Church Cr

Church La

Church

Harbour

Pier (dis)

Pier

Limekilns Harbour

Ramsay La

Red

Charlestown

Stepping Stones

Square D4
1 Capernaum Court
2 Mylneburn Gardens
3 Orchard Square

Firth of Forth

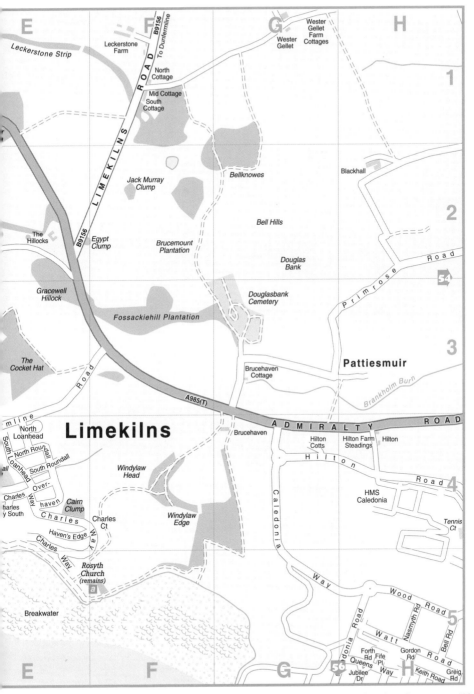

E   F   G   H

1

Leckerstone Strip

Leckerstone Farm

North Cottage

Mid Cottage
South Cottage

B9156
To Dunfermline

Wester Gellet Farm Cottages

Wester Gellet

Blackhall

1

Jack Murray Clump

Bellknowes

2

Bell Hills

The Hillocks

Egypt Clump

Brucemount Plantation

Douglas Bank

Primrose Road

54

Gracewell Hillock

Douglasbank Cemetery

Fossackiehill Plantation

3

The Cocket Hat

Road

Brucehaven Cottage

Pattiesmuir

Brankholm Burn

A985(T)

ADMIRALTY ROAD

North Loanhead

Limekilns

Brucehaven

Hilton Cotts

Hilton Farm Steadings

Hilton

Hilton Road

South Loanhead
North Roundall
South Roundall

Over-
haven
Cairn Clump

Windylaw Head

Caledonia

HMS Caledonia

4

Charles Way
Charles South

Charles

Charles Ct

Windylaw Edge

Tennis Ct

Haven's Edge

Charles Way

Rosyth Church (remains)

a

Way

Wood Road

5

Breakwater

Caledonia Road

Watt

Nasmyth Rd

Bell Rd

Road

56

Forth Rd
Queens Way

Fife Pl

Jubilee Dr

Gordon Rd

Keith Road

Greig Rd

G   H

E   F   G   H

Index to street names can be found starting on page 102

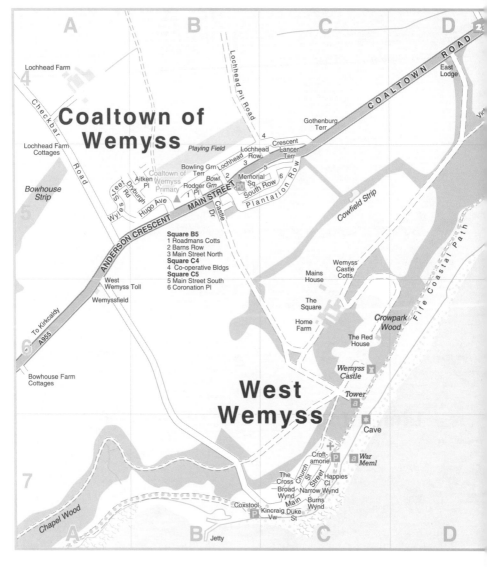

Index to Coaltown of, East & West Wemyss

Aitken Place	B5	Bowling Green Terrace	B5	Church Street	C7	Glebe Park
Alexander Street	F1	Braehead	E3	Co-operative	C4	Gothenburg Terrace
Anderson Crescent	A5	Broad Wynd	C7	Buildings (4)		Grieve Grove
Approach Row	E4	Burns Wynd	C7	Coronation Place (6)	C5	Happies Close
Approach Terrace	E3	Burt's Wynd	E2	Coxstool	B7	Haugh, The
Back Dykes	E4	Castle Drive	B5	Croftamorie	C7	Hendrie Court
Barns Row (2)	B5	Castleton Court	D3	Cross, The	C7	Hendrie Crescent
Barony, The	F2	Cave Cottages	F3	Dryburgh Road	B5	Hendrie Lane
Bowhouse Farm Cottages	A6	Checkbar Road	A4	Duke Street	C7	Hendrie Place
				East Brae	F3	High Road
				Fife Coastal Path	D6	Hugo Avenue

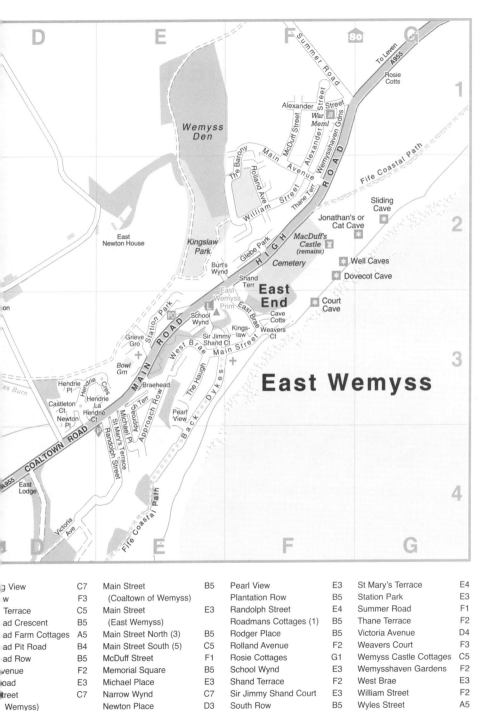

East Wemyss

East End

Wemyss Den

East Newton House

Kingslaw Park

Bowl Grn

Braehead

Castleton Ct

Newton Pl

Hendrie Pl

Hendrie La

Hendrie Ct

Cres

East Lodge

Victoria Ave

Sliding Cave

Jonathan's or Cat Cave

MacDuff's Castle (remains)

Well Caves

Dovecot Cave

Cemetery

Court Cave

Cave Cotts

Weavers Ct

Rosie Cotts

To Leven A955

Fife Coastal Path

Fife Coastal Path

Summer Road

Alexander Street

McDuff Street

Alexander Street

War Meml

Main Avenue

Thane Terr

Wemysshaven Gdns

The Barony

Rolland Ave

William Street

Glebe Park

HIGH ROAD

Burt's Wynd

Shand Terr

East Wemyss Prim

School Wynd

Sir Jimmy Shand Ct

Kingslaw

East Brae

Grieve Gro

Station Park

MAIN ROAD

West Brae

The Haugh

Main Street

Back Dykes

Pearl View

ch Terr

Michael Pl

choiddy

St Mary's Terrace

Approach Row

Randolph Street

COALTOWN ROAD

A955

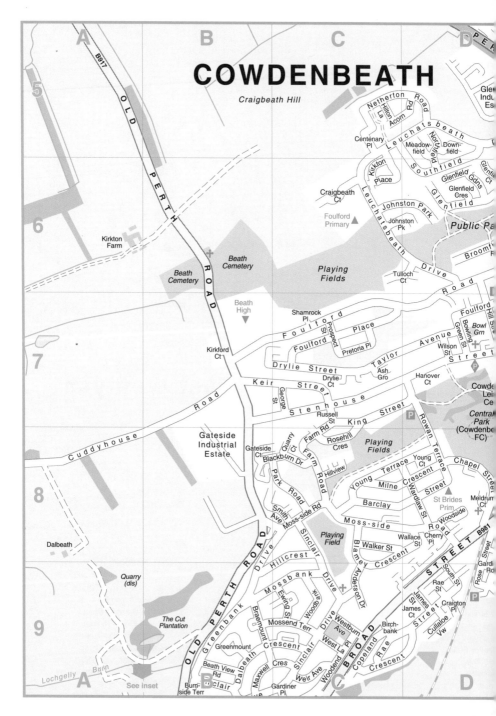

COWDENBEATH

Craigbeath Hill

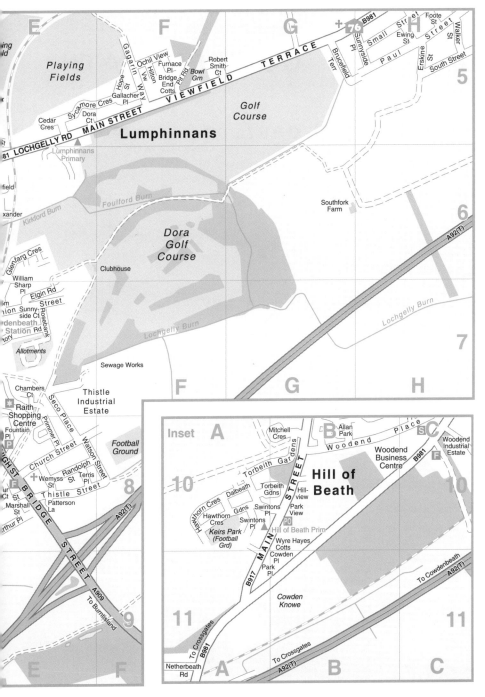

Index to street names can be found on page 98

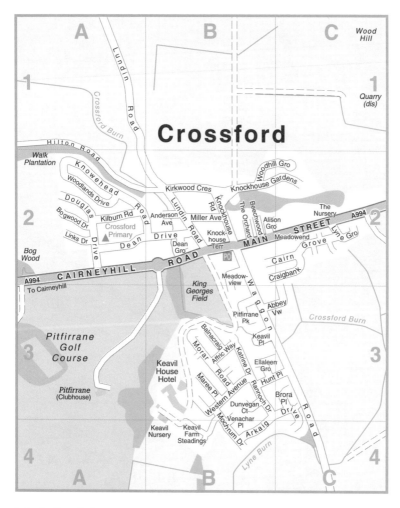

Index to Crossford

Abbey View	B3	Ellaleen Grove	B3	Maree Place	B3
Affric Way	B3	Hilton Road	A1	Meadowend	C2
Alison Grove	B2	Hunt Place	B3	Meadowview	B2
Anderson Avenue	B2	Katrine Drive	B3	Miller Avenue	B2
Arkaig Drive	B4	Keavil Farm Steadings	B4	Mochrum Drive	B3
Balnacraig	B3	Keavil Place	B3	Morar Road	B3
Beechwood	B2	Kilburn Road	A2	Nursery, The	C2
Bogwood Drive	A2	Kirkwood Crescent	B2	Orchard, The	B2
Brora Place	C3	Knockhouse Gardens	B2	Pitfirrane Park	B3
Cairn Grove	C2	Knockhouse Road	B2	Rannoch Drive	B3
Cairneyhill Road	A2	Knockhouse Terrace	B2	Venachar Place	B3
Craigbank	C2	Knowehead Road	A2	Waggon Road	B2
Dean Drive	A2	Links Drive	A2	Western Avenue	B3
Dean Grove	B2	Lundin Road	A1, B2	Woodhill Grove	B2
Douglas Drive	A2	Lyne Grove	C2	Woodlands Drive	A2
Dunvegan Court	B3	Main Street	B2		

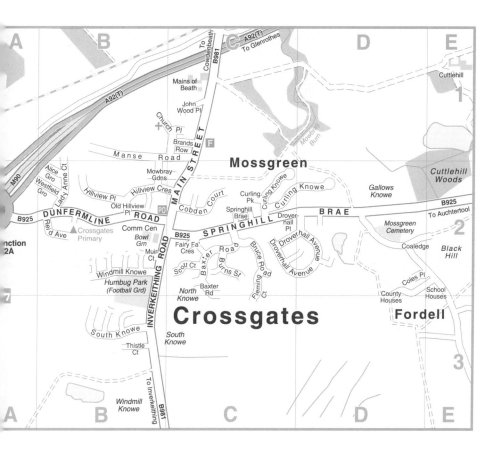

Index to Crossgates

Alice Grove	B2	Hillview Place	B2
Baxter Road	C2	Inverkeithing Road	B3
Brands Row	C1	John Wood Place	C1
Bruce Road	C2	Lady Anne Court	B2
Burns Street	C2	Main Street	C2
Church Place	B1	Manse Road	B1
Coaledge	D2	Mowbray Gardens	B2
Cobden Court	C2	Muir Court	B2
Coles Place	D2	Old Hillview Place	B2
County Houses	D3	Reid Avenue	B2
Curling Knowe	C2	School Houses	E2
Curling Park	C2	Scott Court	C2
Droverhall Avenue	C2	South Knowe	B3
Droverhall Place	C2	Springhill Brae	C2
Dunfermline Road	B2	Thistle Court	B3
Fairy Fa' Crescent	C2	Westfield Grove	B2
Fleming Court	C2	Windmill Knowe	B2
Hillview Crescent	B2		

 ## CULROSS & VALLEYFIELD

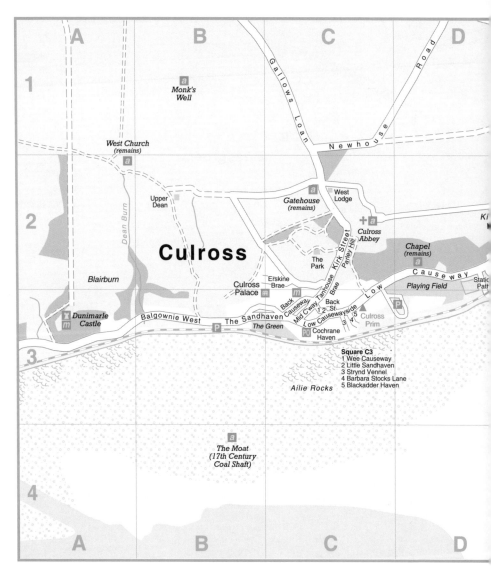

Square C3
1 Wee Causeway
2 Little Sandhaven
3 Strynd Vennel
4 Barbara Stocks Lane
5 Blackadder Haven

Index to Culross & Valleyfield

Abbey Street	G1	Burns Street		F1	Dunimarle Street
Back Causeway	C3	Carlyle Street		G1	Durham Terrace
Back Street	C3	Catherines Wynd		E1	Erskine Brae
Balgownie West	B3	Chapel Place		G1	Forth Crescent
Barbara Stocks Lane (4)	C3	Chapel Street		G1	Forth View Cottages
Beech Place	F2	Chapel Terrace		G1	Forthbank Place
Beveridge Cottages	H2	Clinkum Bank		H1	Gallows Loan
Blackadder Haven (5)	C3	Cochrane Haven		C3	Greenbank
		Cormailin Place		G1	Hamilton Terrace
		Daly Gardens		E1	Kinloss Court

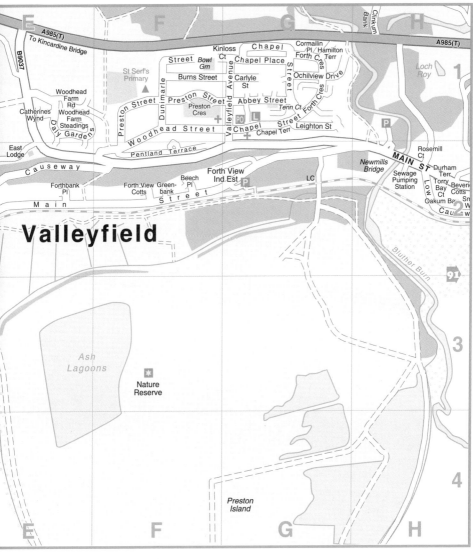

Valleyfield

k Street	C2	Parley Hill	C2
ghton Street	G2	Pentland Terrace	F2
e Sandhaven (2)	C3	Preston Crescent	F1
w Causeway	C3	Preston Street	F1
w Causewayside	C3	Rosemill Court	H2
n Street (Low Torry)	H2	Sandhaven, The	B2
n Street (Valley)	E2	Smiddy Wynd	H2
Causeway	C3	Station Path	D2
vhouse Road	C1	Strynd Vennel (3)	C3
nilview Drive	G1	Tanhouse Brae	C3

Torry Bay Court	H2
Valleyfield Avenue	G2
Veere Park	D2
Wee Causeway (1)	C3
Woodhead Farm Road	E1
Woodhead Farm Steadings	E1
Woodhead Street	F1

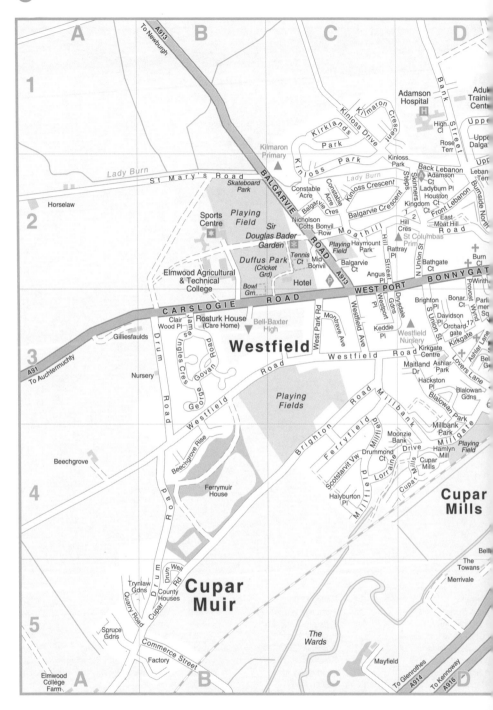

A913
To Newburgh

A

B

C

D

1

Adamson Hospital

Bank Street

Adult Training Centre

High St
Cl

Upper

Kilmaron
Primary

Kirklands

Park

Kilmaron Crescent

Kinloss Drive

Rose
Terr

Upper
Dalga

Lady Burn

St Mary's Road

BALGARVIE

Kinloss

Park

Kinloss
Park

Back Lebanon
Adamson
Ct

Lebanon
Terr

Upr

Horselaw

Skateboard
Park

Constable
Acre

Lady Burn

Kinloss Crescent

Constable
Acre

Balgarvie
Acre

Steps
Skinners

Ladyburn Pl
Houston
Kingdom Ct

Burnside North

2

Sports
Centre

Playing
Field

Sir
Douglas Bader
Garden

ROAD

Balgarvie Cres

Nicholson
Cotts Bonvil
Row

Balgarvie Crescent

Hill
Cres

Front Lebanon

East
Moat Hill
Road

Cl
Row

Moat hill

St Columbas
Prim

Elmwood Agricultural
& Technical
College

Duffus Park
(Cricket
Grd)

Tennis
Ct

Mid
Bonvil

Playing
Field

Haymount
Park

Rattray
Pl

St Columbas
Prim

Street

Bathgate
Ct

Burn
Cl

Bowl
Grn

Hotel

Balgarvie
Ct

Angus
Pl

N Union

BONNYGAT

P

A913

WEST PORT

Provost Wynd
Winth.

Bonar.
Pl

Parli
mer
Sq

CARSLOGIE

ROAD

Westfield Ave

West Park Rd

Montrave Ave

Westport
Pl

Drysdale
Gdns

Brighton
Pl

S Union St

Davidson
Pl

Provost Wynd

Ct

Clair
Wood Pl

Rosturk House
(Care Home)

Bell-Baxter
High

Keddie
Pl

Westfield
Nursery

Orchard
gate
Kirkgate

Ashlar Lane

Gilliesfaulds

James
Road

Ingles Cres

Govan

Drum Road

Westfield

Westfield Road

Westfield Road

Kirkgate
Centre

Lovers Lane

Bel

3

A91
To Auchtermuchty

Nursery

George
Road

Maitland
Dr

Ashlar
Park

Hackston
Pl

Blalowan
Park

Bel

Westfield
Road

Playing
Fields

Road

Millbank

Blalowan
Gdns

Road

Beechgrove

Beechgrove Rise

Brighton
Road

Ferryfield

Millfield

Drummond
Ct

Moonzie
Bank

Millbank
Park

Drive

Millgate

Hamlyn
Mill

Playing
Field

4

Ferrymuir
House

Scotstarvit Vw

Millfield

Lorraine

Cupar
Mills

**Cupar
Mills**

Halyburton
Pl

Cupar

Road

Bell

The
Towans

Merrivale

Trynlaw
Gdns

Drum Well
Rd

County
Houses

**Cupar
Muir**

Cupar
Drum

Spruce
Gdns

Quarry Road

The
Wards

5

Commerce Street

Factory

Mayfield

Elmwood
College
Farm

A

B

C

To Glenrothes

A914

To Kennoway

A916

D

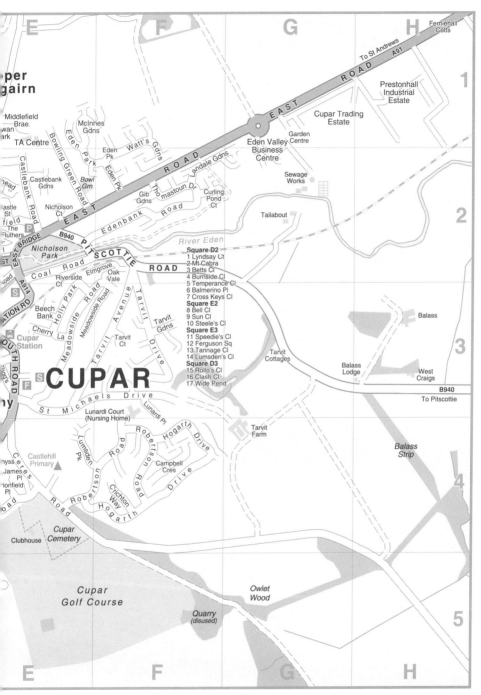

Square D2
1 Lyndsay Ct
2 Mt-Cabra
3 Betts Cl
4 Burnside Cl
5 Temperance Cl
6 Balmerino Pl
7 Cross Keys Cl
Square E2
8 Bell Cl
9 Sun Cl
10 Steele's Cl
Square E3
11 Speedie's Cl
12 Ferguson Sq
13 Tannage Cl
14 Lumsden's Cl
Square D3
15 Rollo's Cl
16 Clash Cl
17 Wide Pend

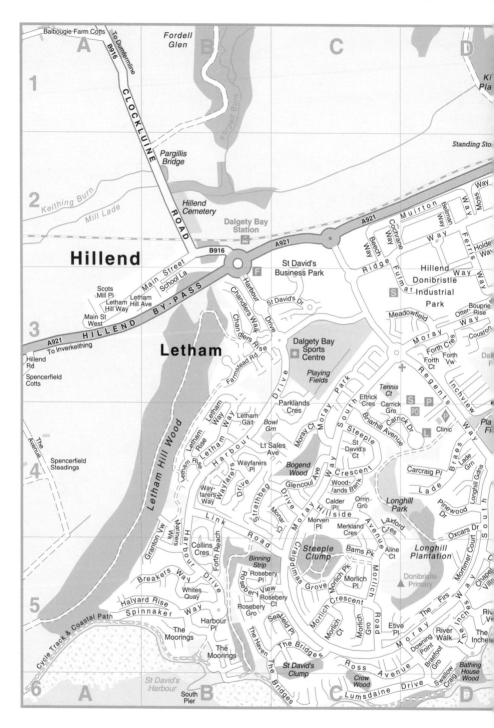

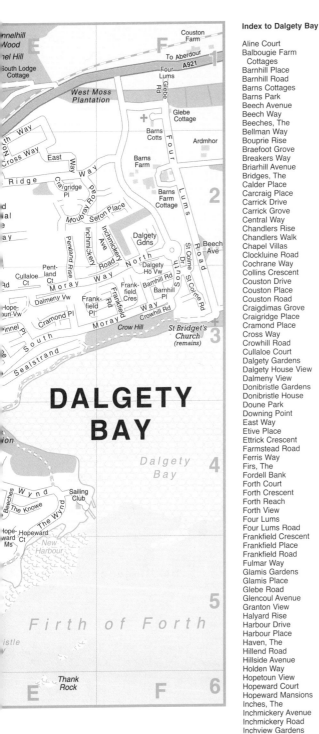

Index to Dalgety Bay

Aline Court	C5
Balbougie Farm Cottages	A1
Barnhill Place	F3
Barnhill Road	F3
Barns Cottages	F2
Barns Park	C5
Beech Avenue	F2
Beech Way	C2
Beeches, The	E4
Bellman Way	D2
Bouprie Rise	D3
Braefoot Grove	D5
Breakers Way	B5
Briarhill Avenue	C4
Bridges, The	C6
Calder Place	C4
Carcraig Place	D4
Carrick Drive	C4
Carrick Grove	C4
Central Way	E2
Chandlers Rise	B3
Chandlers Walk	B3
Chapel Villas	D5
Clockluine Road	A1
Cochrane Way	C2
Collins Crescent	B5
Couston Drive	D3
Couston Place	D3
Couston Road	D3
Craigdimas Grove	C5
Craigridge Place	E2
Cramond Place	E3
Cross Way	E2
Crowhill Road	F3
Cullaloe Court	E3
Dalgety Gardens	F2
Dalgety House View	F2
Dalmeny View	E3
Donibristle Gardens	D5
Donibristle House	D5
Doune Park	E3
Downing Point	D5
East Way	E2
Etive Place	C5
Ettrick Crescent	C3
Farmstead Road	B3
Ferris Way	D2
Firs, The	D5
Fordell Bank	E3
Forth Court	D3
Forth Crescent	D3
Forth Reach	B5
Forth View	D3
Four Lums	F1
Four Lums Road	F2
Frankfield Crescent	F3
Frankfield Place	E3
Frankfield Road	F3
Fulmar Way	D3
Glamis Gardens	D4
Glamis Place	D4
Glebe Road	F1
Glencoul Avenue	C4
Granton View	B5
Halyard Rise	B5
Harbour Drive	B3, B5
Harbour Place	B5
Haven, The	B5
Hillend Road	A3
Hillside Avenue	C4
Holden Way	D2
Hopetoun View	E3
Hopeward Court	E4
Hopeward Mansions	E5
Inches, The	D5
Inchmickery Avenue	F2
Inchmickery Road	E2
Inchview Gardens	D3
Knowe, The	E4
Lade Braes	D4
Lade Green	D4
Laxford Crescent	C4
Letham Gait	B4
Letham Hill Avenue	A3
Letham Hill Way	A3
Letham Rise	B4
Letham Way	B4
Link Road	B4
Longhill Gardens	D4
Lt Sales Avenue	C4
Lumsdaine Drive	C6
Main Street West	A3
Main Street	B3
Mariners Walk	B5
Markfield Road	E3
Meadowfield	D3
Merkland Crescent	C4
Merlin Way	E2
Monar Court	C5
Moorings, The	B5
Moray Court	C4
Moray Park	C4
Moray Way	F3
Moray Way North	D3
Moray Way South	C4, D4
Morlich Court	C5
Morlich Crescent	C5
Morlich Grove	C5
Morlich Park	C5
Morlich Place	C5
Morlich Road	C5
Mortimer Court	D5
Morven Place	C4
Moss Way	D2
Moubray Road	E2
Muirton Way	D2
North Way	E2
Orrin Grove	C4
Otterston Grove	D3
Oxcars Drive	D4
Parklands Crescent	C3
Pentland Court	E3
Pentland Rise	E2
Pinewood Drive	D4
Pinnel Place	E3
Regents Way	D3
Ridge Way	C2, E2
River View	D5
River Walk	D5
Rosebery Court	B5
Rosebery Grove	B5
Rosebery Place	B5
Rosebery View	B5
Ross Avenue	C5
St Bridgets Brae	E3
St Colme Drive	F2
St Colme Road	F3
St David's Court	C4
St David's Drive	C3
School Lane	B3
Scots Mill Place	A3
Seafield Place	C5
Sealstrand	E3
Seton Place	F2
Spencerfield Cottages	A3
Spencerfield Steadings	A3
Spinnaker Way	B5
Spinneys, The	E4
Steeple Crescent	C4
Strathbeg Drive	B4
Swallow Craig	D6
Taxi Way	D2
Wayfarers Drive	B4
Wayfarers Place	B4
Wayfarers Way	B4
West Way	D2
Whites Quay	B5
Woodlands Bank	C4
Wynd, The	E4

Index to Dunfermline

Abbey Park Place	E6	Backwell Court	B4	Blackwood Gardens	K10	Buchanan Street	E6
Abbey View	J7	Baldridge Place	E2	Blackwood Green	K10	Buckyburn Place	J3
Abbot Street (4)	E6	Baldridgeburn	C4	Blackwood Way	K10	Buffies Brae	D5
Abel Place	K5	Balfour Court	H4	Blair Drive	F3	Burns Street	C4
Aberdour Crescent	H8	Balvaird Place	G3	Blake Street	G8	Burt Grove	J8
Aberdour Place	H8	Bannerman Street	E4	Bleachfield Court	J6	Burt Street	E3
Aberdour Road	G8, L9	Bannoch Brae	G6	Blelloch's Close (1)	D6	Bute Crescent	J6
Abington Road	D7	Barbour Grove	C4	Bonnar Street	E5	Cadell Reach	L10
Adamson Crescent	G4	Barrie Place	C4	Bonnyton Place	H6	Cairncubie Road	G1
Afton Grove	K4	Barrie Street	C4	Bothwell Court	E7	Caithness Drive	N8
Albany Street	F5	Beath View	J5	Bothwell Street	F7	Caledonia House	J10
Alder Grove	H8	Beatty Place	G4	Bow Butts	E7	Calais View	K8
Alderston Drive	H3	Beauly Crescent	N9	Bracklinn Brae	C4	Calaisburn Cottages	L8
Alexander Way	M9	Beck Crescent	G4	Braemar Drive	L5	Calaisburn Place	J8
Alexandra Street	E4	Beech Grove	H9	Braemar Gardens	L5	Callander Terrace	L5
Alford Way	L5	Beldorney Place	H3	Braigh Gardens	B3	Cameron Street	C5
Alice Cox Walk	F8	Bellyeoman Lane	G4	Brambling Road	L7	Campbell Street	E5
Allan Crescent	J7	Bellyeoman Road	F5	Briar Place	G6	Canmore Grove	F3
Allan Lea Terrace	D4	Bendachin Drive	J4	Bridge Street	D6	Canmore Street	E6
Almond Road	J7	Bennachie Way	M8	Bridges View	K3	Canmore Terrace	E2
Alness Grove	D7	Bergen Avenue	L7	Brodick Gardens	K5	Canon Lynch Court	D5
Annfield Farm Road	M10	Bernard Shaw Street	C4	Brodie Walk	L5	Carlyle Lane	C4
Appin Crescent	F5	Berrylaw Place	C5	Broom Grove	K9	Carnbee Place	G5
Ardeer Place	G7	Berrylaw Road	C5	Broomfield Drive	E4	Carnegie Avenue	J10
Ariston Road	K5	Beveridge Street	G7	Broomhead Drive	D4	Carnegie Court	E5
Arthur Street	E4	Birch Grove	H9	Broomhead Park	D4	Carnegie Drive	E5
Ash Grove	H9	Birnam Gardens	L5	Broomieknowe	G6	Carnock Road	A3
Athol Place	G5	Birrell Drive	G8	Broomknowe Terrace	E3	Carron Lane	K5
Avens Close	D4	Bittern Court	L7	Bruce Gardens	L9	Carswell Place	D3
Aytoun Grove	C4	Blackburn Avenue	B3	Bruce Street	D5	Castings, The	A3
		Blacklaw Road	G6	Brucefield Avenue	F7	Castle Brae	K10
		Blackwood Court	K10	Brucefield Feus	G6	Castle Row	A3

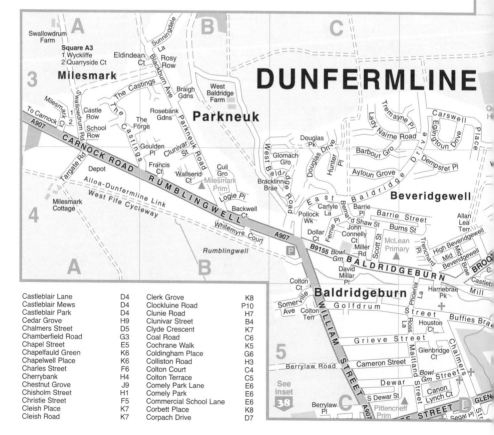

Castleblair Lane	D4	Clerk Grove	K8
Castleblair Mews	D4	Clockluine Road	P10
Castleblair Park	D4	Clunie Road	H7
Cedar Grove	H9	Clunivar Street	B4
Chalmers Street	D5	Clyde Crescent	K7
Chamberfield Road	G3	Coal Road	C6
Chapel Street	E5	Cochrane Walk	K5
Chapelfauld Green	K6	Coldingham Place	G6
Chapelwell Place	K6	Colliston Road	H3
Charles Street	F6	Colton Court	C4
Cherrybank	H4	Colton Terrace	C5
Chestnut Grove	J9	Comely Park Lane	E6
Chisholm Street	H1	Comely Park	E6
Christie Street	F5	Commercial School Lane	E6
Cleish Place	K7	Corbett Place	K8
Cleish Road	K7	Corpach Drive	D7

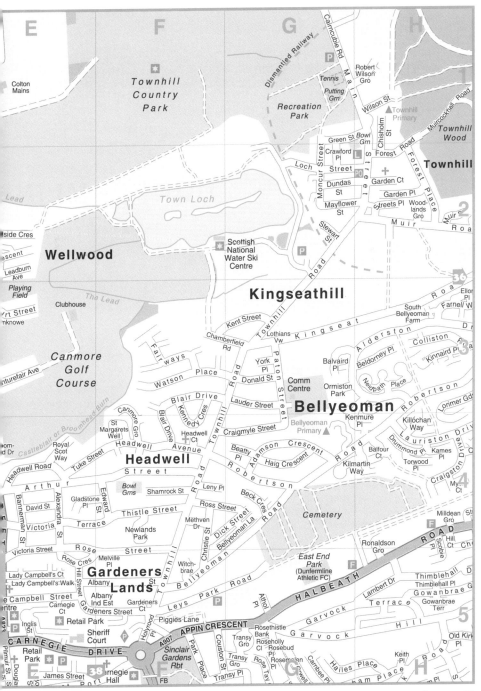

Colton
Mains

Townhill
Country
Park

Recreation
Park

Cairncubie Rd

Dismantled Railway

P

Tennis

Putting
Grn

Robert
Wilson
Gro

Wilson St

▲Townhill
Primary

Muircockhall Road

Townhill
Wood

Townhill

Lead

Town Loch

Green St
Bowl
Grn

Crawford
Pl

Forest Road

Chisholm
St

Forest Place

Muir
Road

Loch
Street

Moncur Street

L

Dundas
St

Garden Ct

Garden Pl

Muir

Mayflower
St

streets Pl

Wood-
lands
Gro

iside Cres

scent

Wellwood

Leadburn
Ave

Playing
Field

rt Street

nknowe

Scottish
National
Water Ski
Centre

P

Stewart St

Road

Road

Ellor
Pl

Farneil W

Kingseathill

The Lead

Clubhouse

Kent Street

Chamberfield
Rd

Townhill Road

Lothians
Vw

Kingseat

South
Bellyeoman
Farm

Dr

Alderston

Colliston

Canmore
Golf
Course

Fairways

Watson
Place

York
Pl

Donald St

Paton Road

Comm
Centre

Balvaird
Pl

Beldorney Pl

Neidpath Place

Kinnaird Pl

Robertson

turefair Ave

Blair Drive

Kennedy Cres

Lauder Street

Ormiston
Park

Bellyeoman

Kenmure
Pl

Killóchan
Way

Lorimer Gdr

om-
d Dr

Castleblair or Broomhead Burn

St
Margarets
Well

Canmore Gro

Blair Drive

Headwell
Ct

Craigmyle Street

Bellyeoman
Primary ▲

Lauriston Driv

Drummond Pl

Kames
Pl

Craigston Drive

Headwell Road

Royal
Scot
Way

Tuke Street

Headwell

Headwell

Avenue

Townhill Road

Beatty
Pl

Adamson

Crescent

Balfour
Ct

Torwood
Pl

My
Ct

Street

Haig Crescent

Kilmartin
Way

Arthur

Bannerman St

Alexandra St

Gladstone
Pl

Edward

Bowl
Grns

Shamrock St

Leny Pl

Robertson

Road

David St

Victoria
St

Terrace

Thistle Street

Ross Street

Beck Cres

Cemetery

Milldean St
Gro

Hill
Ct
Ch

Newlands
Park

Methven
Dr

Dick Street

Christie St

Bellyeoman La

Ronaldson
Gro

Scobie
Pl

Victoria Street

Rose
Cres

Rose

Street

Melville
St

Witch-
brae

Bellyeoman

Road

East End
Park
(Dunfermline
Athletic FC)

F

ROAD

Thimblehall
Pl

Thimblehall Pl

D

Lady Campbell's Ct

Lady Campbell's Walk

Gardeners
Lands

Albany
St

Leys Park Road

P

Athol
Pl

HALBEATH

Lambert Dr

Terrace

Gowanbrae G

Gowanbrae
Terr

e Campbell Street

Carnegie
Ct

Albany
Ind Est

Gardeners
Ct

Garvock

Hill

ntre

P

Inglis
St

Retail Park

Gardeners Street

Piggies Lane

Holyrood

APPIN CRESCENT

A907

Rosethistle
Bank

Garvock

Old Kirk
Pl

CARNEGIE

Sheriff
Court

P

Sinclair
Gardens
Rbt

Park Place

Couston St

Transy
Gro

Roseholly
Cl

Rosebud

Rose Taylor

Transy
Gro

Rosebud
Pl

Rosemelen

Keith
Pl

Hailes Place

Plimuir St

Retail
Park

DRIVE

James Street

arnegie
Hall

FB

Transy Pl

well

nbee Pl

am Place

H

Pl

Douglas

38

Port Hall

Index to street names is continued on page 37

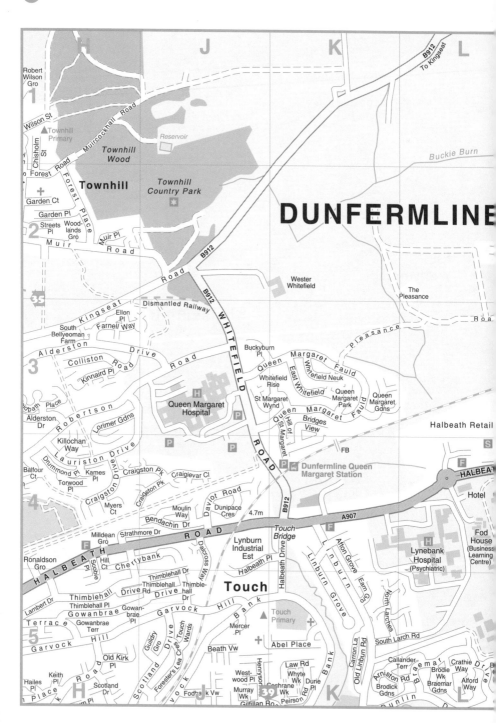

DUNFERMLINE

Townhill

Townhill Wood

Townhill Country Park

Robert Wilson Gro

Wilson St

Chisholm St

Forest

Garden Ct

Garden Pl

Streets Pl

Woodlands Gro

Muir Pl

Muir Road

Forest Place Road

Muircockhall Road

Reservoir

B912

To Kingseat

Buckie Burn

Wester Whitefield

The Pleasance

Roa

Dismantled Railway

Kingseat

Ellon Pl

Farnell Way

South Bellyeoman Farm

Alderston

Colliston Road

Kinnaird Pl

Drive

Road

WHITEFIELD

Pleasance

Buckyburn Pl

Queen Margaret Fauld

Whitefield Neuk

Whitefield Rise

East Whitefield

St Margaret Wynd

Queen Margaret Park

Queen Margaret Gdns

Queen Margaret Fauld

Place

Alderston Dr

Robertson

Lorimer Gdns

Killochan Way

Lauriston Drive

Queen Margaret Hospital

Queen Margaret Hill of

Bridges View

Halbeath Retail

S

F

HALBEA

Balfour Ct

Drummond Pl

Torwood Pl

Kames Pl

Craigston Dr

Craigston Pk

Craigston Pk

Craigievar Cl

FB

Dunfermline Queen Margaret Station

Myers Ct

Moulin Way

Bendachin Dr

Daviot Road

Dunipace Cres

4.7m

B912

A907

Afton Grove

Linburn Grove

Linburn Drive

Earn Gro

Nrth Larches

Hotel

Fod House (Business Learning Centre)

Milldean Gro

Strathmore Dr

Ronaldson Gro

HALBEATH

ROAD

Hill Ct

Scobie

Cherrybank

Dalcross Way

Lynburn Industrial Est

Halbeath Pl

Touch Bridge

Lynebank Hospital (Psychiatric)

Lambert Dr

Thimblehall Pl

Thimblehall

Drive Rd

Thimblehall Dr

Thimblehall Drive

Thimblehall Dr

Touch

Gowanbrae

Gowanbrae Pl

Gowanbrae Terr

Terrace

Garvock Hill

Garvock Hill

Bank

Touch Wards

Touch Primary

Mercer Pl

Abel Place

South Larch Rd

Carron La

Old Linburn Rd

Callander Terr

Aniston Rd

Brodie Wk

Braemar Gdns

Crathie Way

Alford Way

Braemar

Old Kirk Pl

Hailes Pl

Keith Pl

Scotland Dr

Road

Scotland Drive

Guildry Gro

Foresters Lea Cres

Garvock Hill

Beath Vw

Westwood Pl

Henryson

Murray Wk

Fodha k Vw

Gilfillan Ro

Peirson

Law Rd

Whyte Wk

Cochrane Wk

Durie Pl

Brodick Gdns

39

H

J

K

L

1

2

35

3

4

5

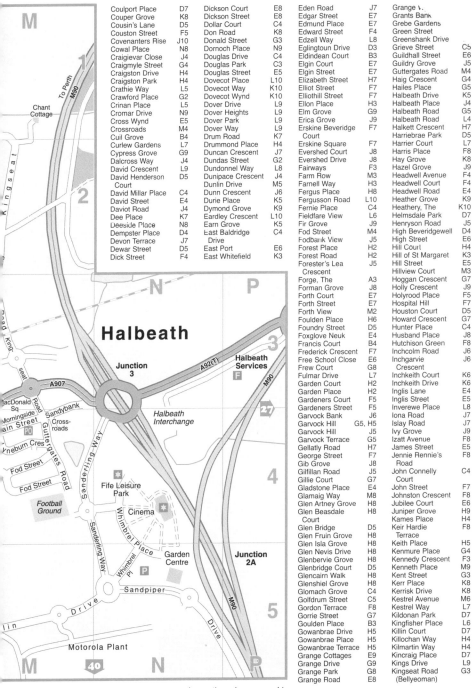

Coulport Place	D7	Dickson Court	E8
Couper Grove	K8	Dickson Street	E8
Cousin's Lane	D5	Dollar Court	C4
Couston Street	F5	Don Road	K8
Covenanters Rise	J10	Donald Street	G3
Cowal Place	N8	Dornoch Place	N9
Craigievar Close	J4	Douglas Drive	C4
Craigmyle Street	G4	Douglas Park	C3
Craigston Drive	H4	Douglas Street	E5
Craigston Park	H4	Dovecot Place	L10
Crathie Way	L5	Dovecot Way	K10
Crawford Place	G2	Dovecot Wynd	K10
Crinan Place	L5	Dover Drive	L9
Cromar Drive	N9	Dover Heights	L9
Cross Wynd	E5	Dover Park	L9
Crossroads	M4	Dover Way	L9
Cuil Grove	B4	Drum Road	K7
Curlew Gardens	L7	Drummond Place	H4
Cypress Grove	G9	Duncan Crescent	J7
Dalcross Way	J4	Dundas Street	G2
David Crescent	L9	Dundonnel Way	L8
David Henderson	D5	Dunipace Crescent	J4
Court		Dunlin Drive	M5
David Millar Place	C4	Dunn Crescent	J6
David Street	E4	Durie Place	K5
Daviot Road	J4	Dymond Grove	K9
Dee Place	K7	Eardley Crescent	L10
Deeside Place	N8	Earn Grove	K5
Dempster Place	D4	East Baldridge	C4
Devon Terrace	J7	Drive	
Dewar Street	D5	East Port	E6
Dick Street	F4	East Whitefield	K3

Eden Road	J7	Grange V.	
Edgar Street	E7	Grants Bank	
Edmund Place	E7	Grebe Gardens	
Edward Street	F4	Green Street	
Edzell Way	L8	Greenshank Drive	
Eglingtoun Drive	D3	Grieve Street	C5
Eldindean Court	B3	Guildhall Street	E6
Elgin Court	E7	Guildry Grove	J5
Elgin Street	E7	Guttergates Road	M4
Elizabeth Street	H7	Haig Crescent	G4
Elliot Street	F7	Hailes Place	G5
Elliothill Street	F7	Halbeath Drive	K5
Ellon Place	H3	Halbeath Place	J4
Elm Grove	G9	Halbeath Road	G5
Erica Grove	J9	Halbeath Road	L4
Erskine Beveridge	F7	Halkett Crescent	H7
Court		Harriebrae Park	D5
Erskine Square	F7	Harrier Court	L7
Evershed Court	J8	Harris Place	F8
Evershed Drive	J8	Hay Grove	K8
Fairways	F3	Hazel Grove	J9
Farm Row	M3	Headwell Avenue	F4
Farnell Way	H3	Headwell Court	F4
Fergus Place	H8	Headwell Road	E4
Fergusson Road	L10	Heather Grove	K9
Fernie Place	C4	Heathery, The	K10
Fieldfare View	L6	Helmsdale Park	D7
Fir Grove	J9	Henryson Road	J5
Fod Street	M4	High Beveridgewell	D4
Fodbank View	J5	High Street	E6
Forest Place	H2	Hill Court	H4
Forest Road	H2	Hill of St Margaret	K3
Forester's Lea	J5	Hill Street	E5
Crescent		Hillview Court	M3
Forge, The	A3	Hoggan Crescent	G7
Forman Grove	J8	Holly Crescent	J9
Forth Court	E7	Holyrood Place	F5
Forth Street	E7	Hospital Hill	F7
Forth View	M2	Houston Court	D5
Foulden Place	H6	Howard Crescent	G7
Foundry Street	D5	Hunter Place	C4
Foxglove Neuk	E4	Husband Place	J8
Francis Court	B4	Hutchison Green	F8
Frederick Street	F7	Inchcolm Road	J6
Free School Close	E6	Inchgarvie	J6
Frew Court	G8	Crescent	
Fulmar Drive	L7	Inchkeith Court	K6
Garden Court	H2	Inchkeith Drive	K6
Garden Place	H2	Inglis Lane	E4
Gardeners Court	F5	Inglis Street	E5
Gardeners Street	F5	Inverewe Place	L8
Garvock Bank	J6	Iona Road	J7
Garvock Hill	G5, H5	Islay Road	J7
Garvock Hill	J5	Ivy Grove	J9
Garvock Terrace	G5	Izatt Avenue	F8
Gellatly Road	H7	James Street	E5
George Street	F7	Jennie Rennie's	F8
Gib Grove	J8	Road	
Gilfillan Road	J5	John Connelly	C4
Gillie Court	G7	Court	
Gladstone Place	E4	John Street	F7
Glamaig Way	M8	Johnston Crescent	F8
Glen Artney Grove	H8	Jubilee Court	E6
Glen Beasdale	H8	Juniper Grove	H9
Court		Kames Place	H4
Glen Bridge	D5	Keir Hardie	F8
Glen Fruin Grove	H8	Terrace	
Glen Isla Grove	H8	Keith Place	H5
Glen Nevis Drive	H8	Kenmure Place	G4
Glenbervie Grove	H8	Kennedy Crescent	F3
Glenbridge Court	D5	Kenneth Place	M9
Glencairn Walk	H8	Kent Street	G3
Glenshiel Grove	H8	Kerr Place	K8
Glomach Grove	C4	Kerrisk Drive	K8
Golfdrum Street	C5	Kestrel Avenue	M6
Gordon Terrace	F8	Kestrel Way	L7
Gorrie Street	G7	Kildonan Park	D7
Goulden Place	B3	Kingfisher Place	L6
Gowanbrae Drive	H5	Killin Court	D7
Gowanbrae Place	H5	Killochan Way	H4
Gowanbrae Terrace	H5	Kilmartin Way	H4
Grange Cottages	E9	Kincraig Place	D7
Grange Drive	G9	Kings Drive	L9
Grange Park	G8	Kingseat Road	G3
Grange Road	E8	(Bellyeoman)	

Index to street names is continued on page 41

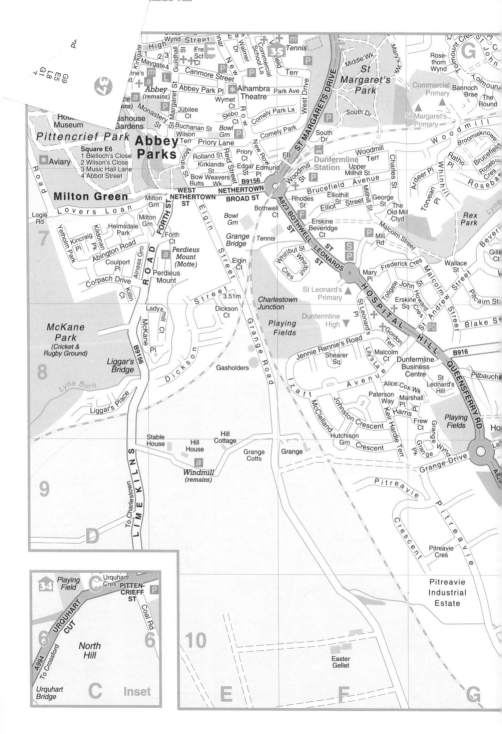

Shaded Areas Done

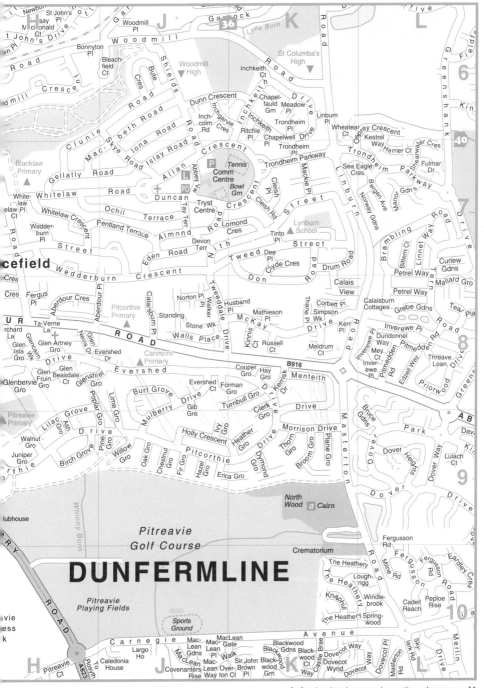

Index to street names is continued on page 41

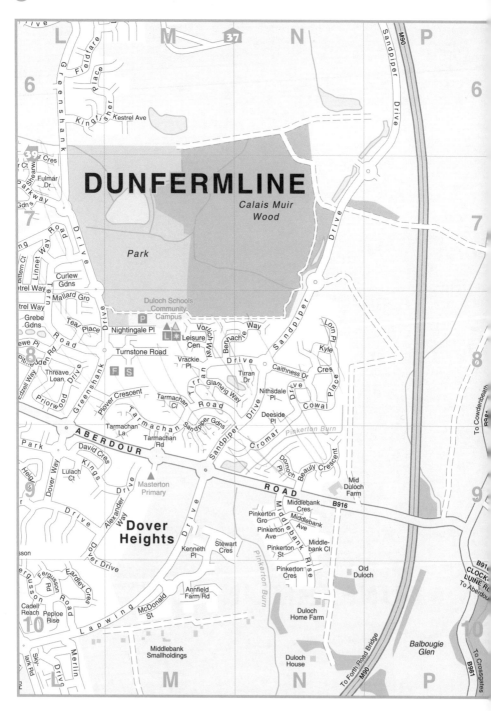

Name	Ref
eat Road	M2
beath)	
ird Place	H3
s Court	K8
nds Street	E6
ate	D6
hill	K10
crescent	N8
num Road	G9
Campbell's	E5
t	
Campbell's	E5
Nairne Road	C3
mill Court	E8
ert Drive	H5
ng Drive	L10
Grove	H9
House	J10
er Street	G3
ton Drive	H4
Road	K5
urn Avenue	E2
ide Crescent	E2
Place	F4
Park Road	F5
's Place	D8
Grove	H9
Lane	F8
Grove	J8
ilns Road	D9
n Grove	K5
n Place	K6
n Road	K4
n Road	K7
ay MacDonald	H6
t	
Way	L7
Street	G2
ead Court	D3
Place	B4
Road	D7
nd Crescent	J7
Row	L2
er Gardens	H3
lace	N8
ns View	G3
rigg	L10
e Street	H7
Loan	D7
Court	L9
urn Crescent	M4
onald Square	M3
lland	F8
cent	
nald Street	M10
he Place	D8
Drive	K8
th Road	H7
e Place	K7
an Gardens	J10
an Gate	J10
an Place	J10
an Walk	J10
an Way	J10
Street	H2
nhill)	
Street	M4
eath)	
nd Street	D5
m Street	G7
d Grove	L8
m Court	F8
Gardens	L7
all Place	F8
lace	F7
Walk	F6
ton Road	K9
son Place	K8
wer Street	G2
te	D6
w Place	K6
w View	M3
m Court	K8
e Place	F5
Menteith Drive	K8
Mercer Place	J5
Merlin Drive	L10
Methven Drive	F4
Mey Court	L8
Mid Beveridgewell	D4
Mid Brae	D4
Middle Walk	F6
Middlebank Avenue	N9
Middlebank Close	N9
Middlebank Crescent	N9
Middlebank Rise	N9
Milesmark Court	A3
Mill Road	F7
Mill Street	D4
Milldean Grove	H4
Miller Road	C4
Millhill Street	F7
Milne Road	L10
Milton Green	E7
Monastery Street	E6
Moncur Street	G2
Moodie Street	E6
Morningside	M4
Morrison Drive	K9
Moulin Way	J4
Muir Place	H2
Muir Road	H2
Muircockhall Road	H1
Mulberry Drive	J9
Murray Walk	J5
Music Hall Lane (3)	E6
Myers Court	H4
Myrtle Wynd	D4
Neidpath Place	H3
Nethertown Broad Street	E7
New Row	E6
Newburn Place	H5
Newlands Park	F4
Nightingale Place	M8
Nith Street	K7
Nithsdale Place	N8
North Larches	K5
Norton Place	J8
Norway Gardens	L7
Oak Grove	J9
Ochil Terrace	J7
Old Kirk Place	H5
Old Kirk Road	G6
Old Linbun Road	K5
Old Mill Courtyard, The	F7
Orchard Lane	H8
Ormiston Park	G3
Orwell Place	G5
Osprey Crescent	L6
Overton Court	J10
Park Avenue	F6
Park Place	F5
Parkneuk Road	B3
Paterson Way	F8
Paton Street	G3
Peirson Road	K5
Peploe Rise	L10
Pentland Terrace	J7
Perdieus Mount	E7
Petrel Way	L8
Phoenix Lane	D5
Piggies Lane	F5
Pilmuir Street	E3
Pilmuir Street	E5
Pine Grove	J9
Pinkerton Avenue	N9
Pinkerton Crescent	N10
Pinkerton Grove	N9
Pinkerton Street	N9
Pitbauchlie Bank	G8
Pitcairn Street	G7
Pitcorthie Drive	H9
Pitcorthie Road	G8
Pitmedden Road	L8
Pitreavie Court	H10
Pitreavie Crescent	G9
Pitreavie Way	G9
Pittencrieff Street	C6
Plane Grove	K9
Pleasance Court	M2
Pleasance Road	K3
Pleasance, The	L2
Plover Crescent	M8
Pollock Walk	C4
Poplar Grove	H8
Priorwood Drive	L8
Priory Court	E6
Priory Lane	E6
Quarryside Court (2)	A3
Queen Anne Street	E5
Queen Margaret Fauld	K3
Queen Margaret Gardens	K3
Queen Margaret Park	K3
Queensferry Road	G8, H10
Ratho Place	G6
Reid Street	E6
Rhodes Street	F7
Ritchie Court	E2
Ritchie Place	K6
Robert Wilson Grove	H1
Robertson Road	G4, H3
Holland Stroot	N9
Ronaldson Grove	H4
Rose Crescent	E5
Rose Street	F5
Rose Tay Court	G5
Rosebank	G7
Rosebank Gardens	B3
Rosebud Place	G5
Rosebush Crescent	G6
Roseholly Close	G5
Rosemalen Place	G5
Rosethistle Bank	G5
Rosethorn Wynd	G6
Ross Lane	D5
Ross Street	F4
Rosy Row	B3
Round, The	G6
Rowan Grove	H8
Royal Scot Way	E4
Rumblingwell	B4
Russell Court	K8
St Andrew Street	G8
St Catherine's Wynd	D6
St John's Drive	G6, H6
St John's Place	H6
St Lawrence Street	G8
St Leonard's Hill	G8
St Leonard's Place	F8
St Leonard's Street	F7
St Margaret Street	E6
St Margaret Wynd	J3
St Margarets Drive	F6
St Margarets Well	F4
Sanderling Way	M4
Sandpiper Drive	N5, M9
Sandpiper Gardens	M9
Sandybank	M4
School Row	A3
Scobie Place	H5
Scotland Drive	H5
Scott Street	C4
Sea Eagle Crescent	L7
Segal Place	D5
Shamrock Street	F4
Shaw Street	H7
Shearer Square	F8
Shearwater Crescent	L7
Shields Road	J6
Simpson Walk	K8
Sir John Brown Place	K10
Skibo Court	E6
Skye Road	J7
Skylark Road	L10
Somerville Avenue	C5
South Dewar Street	C5
South Drive	F6
South Larch Road	K5
Springbank Terrace	E3
Springwood	L10
Spruce Grove	H9
Standing Stone Walk	J8
Stewart Crescent	M9
Stewart Street	G2
Strathmore Drive	H4
Streets Place	H2
Sunningdale Lane	B3
Swallowdrum Road	A3
Sycamore Grove	G9
Targate Road	A4
Tarmachan Close	M8
Tarmachan Lane	M8
Tarmachan Road	M8, M9
Ta-verne Lane	H8
Tay Terrace	J7
Teal Place	L8
Tern Road	L8
Thane Place	K8
Thimblehall Drive	H5
Thimblehall Place	H5
Thimblehall Road	H5
Thistle Street	F4
Thorn Grove	K9
Threave Loan	L8
Tinto Place	K7
Tirran Drive	M8
Tollgate	F7
Tolmount Crescent	G6
Tolmount Drive	G6
Torvean Place	G7
Torwood Place	H4
Touch Wards	J5
Townhill Road	F5, G3
Transy Grove	G5
Transy Place	F5
Tremayne Place	C3
Trenchard Place	D4
Trondheim Parkway	K7
Trondheim Place	K6, K7
Tuke Street	E4
Turnbull Grove	K8
Turnstone Road	M8
Tweed Street	K7
Tweeddale Drive	J8
Upper Millhill Street	F6
Urquhart Crescent	C6
Urquhart Cut	C6
Venturefair Avenue	E3
Victoria Street	E4
Victoria Terrace	E4
Viewfield Terrace	E6
Vorlich Way	M8
Vrackie Place	M8
Walker Place	J8
Wallace Street	G7
Walls Place	J8
Wallsend Court	B4
Walmer Drive	E6
Walnut Grove	H9
Wardlaw Crescent	H8
Watson Place	F3
Wheatear Court	K6
Weavers Walk	E7
Wedderburn Crescent	H7
Wedderburn Place	H7
Wedderburn Street	H7
West Baldridge Road	B4
West Drive	F6
West Nethertown	E7
Street	
Westwood Place	J5
Whimbrel Place	N4, N5
Whinhill	G7
Whirlbut Crescent	F7
Whirlbut Street	F7
Whitefield Neuk	K3
Whitefield Rise	K3
Whitefield Road	J2
Whitelaw Court	H7
Whitelaw Crescent	H7
Whitelaw Place	H7
Whitelaw Road	H7
Whitemyre Court	B4
Whyte Walk	K5
William Street	C5
Willow Grove	J9
Wilson Street	H1
Wilson Terrace	E6
Wilson's Close (2)	E6
Windlebrook	L10
Winterthur Lane	D5
Witchbrae	F5
Woodlands Grove	H2
Woodmill Crescent	H6
Woodmill Place	J6
Woodmill Road	G6, J6
Woodmill Street	F7
Woodmill Terrace	F6
Woodruff Gait	D4
Wyckliffe (1)	A3
Wymet Court	E6
Yetholm Park	D7
York Place	G3

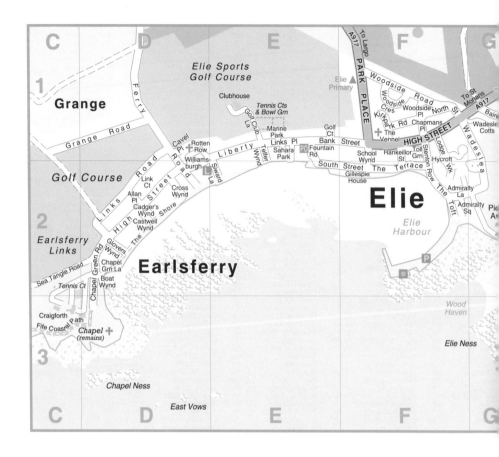

Index to Elie

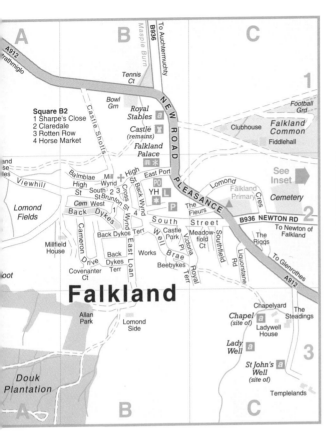

Index to Falkland & Newton of Falkland

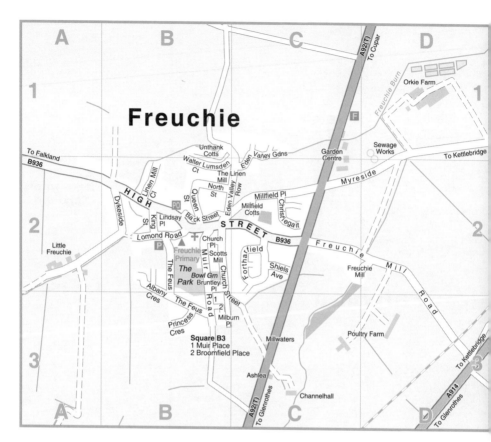

Index to Freuchie

Albany Crescent	B2
Back Street	B2
Broomfield Place (2)	B3
Bruntley Place	B2
Christiegait	C2
Church Place	B2
Church Street	B2
Dykeside	B2
Eden Valley Gardens	C1
Eden Valley Row	B2
Feus, The	B3
Fortharfield	C2
Freuchie Mill Road	D2
Freuchie Mill	C2
High Street	B2
King Street	B2
Lindsay Place	B2
Linen Mill Close	B2
Linen Mill, The	B2
Lomond Road	B2
Milburn Place	B3
Millfield Cottages	C2
Millfield Place	C2
Muir Place (1)	B3
Muir Road	B2
Myreside	C2
North Street	B2
Princess Crescent	B3
Queen Street	B2
Scotts Mill	B2
Shiels Avenue	C2
Unthank Cottages	B1
Walter Lumsden Court	B2

Index to Gauldry

Balgove Avenue	B2
Balgove Road	B2
Bridieswell Gardens	B2
Cherry Grove	B2
Cherry Lane	B2
Crawford Avenue	C2
Hays Road	A2
Kilmany Road	B2
Main Road	A2
Maryknowe	A2
Pitmossie Place	B2
Priory Lane	C2
Priory Road	C2
Quality Street	B2
Windmill Road	B2
Woodend Cottages	C2
Woodend Road	B2

Index to Guardbridge

Ashgrove Buildings	A6
Ashgrove Terrace	A6
Cupar Road	A7
Innerbridge Street	A5
Kinnear Court	B7
McGregors Buildings	A6
Main Street	A5
Miltonbank Crescent	A4
Motray Crescent	A4
Motray Park	A5
Old St Andrews Road	B7
River Terrace	A5
Toll Road	A4

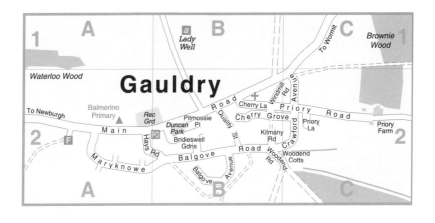

Gauldry

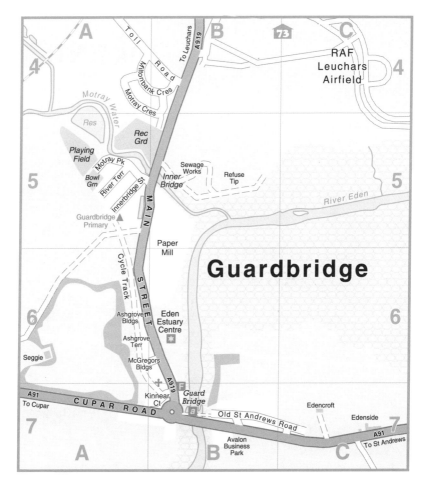

Guardbridge

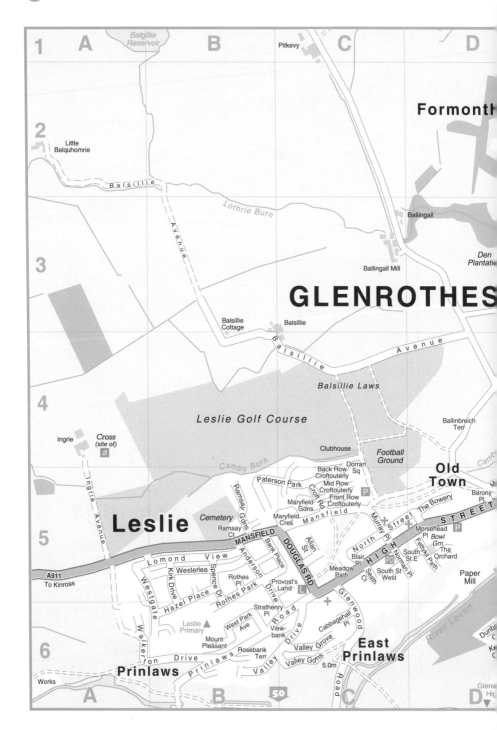

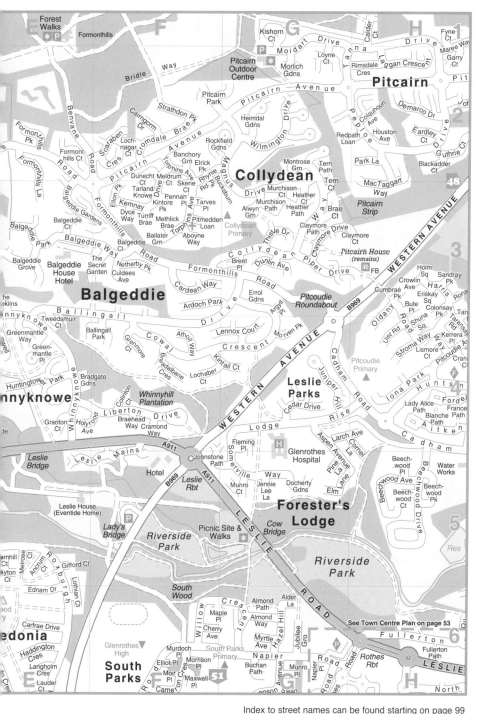

Forest Walks
Formonthills

Kishorn Ct
Fyne Ct
Maree Way
Garry Ct

Moidart Drive
Calder Ct
Loyne Ct
Rimsdale Cres
Laggan Crescent

Pitcairn Outdoor Centre
Morlich Gdns
Pit

Bridle Way
Pitcairn Avenue
Pitcairn

Pitcairn Park
Heimdal Gdns
Wilmington Drive
Colquhoun Ave
Demarco Dr

Strathdon Pk
Cairngorm Dr
Cromdale Brae
Rockfield Gdns
Redpath Loan
Houston Ave
Eardley Ct
Guthrie Ct

Formon Hills Pk
Benvane
Scaraben Cres
Lochnagar Ct
Avenue
Banchory Grn
Elrick Pk
Collydean
Montrose Grn
Tern Path
Park La
Tern Ct
Blackadder Ct

Formont-hills Ct
Pitcairn Road
Dunecht Meldrum Ct
Skene Ct
Rhynie Ct
Buckshurn
Murchison Ct
Heather Ct
MacTaggart Way
48

Formonthills Road
Tophins Ave
Elrick Pk
Magnus Rd
Murchison Grn
Heather Path
Brae Ct
Pitcairn Strip

Formonthills La
Balgeddie Gardens
Tarland Knowe
Kemnay
Kintore Pl
Tarves Pl
Alwyn Grn
Heather Path
Claymore Drive

Balgeddie Ct
Formonthills
Pennan Brae
Methlick Brae
Pitmedden Loan
Thistle Dr
Claymore Path
Claymore Ct

Balgeddie Park
Dyce Way
Turriff Brae
Tophins
Collydean Primary
Claymore Ct

Balgeddie Grove
Balgeddie Cl
Ballater Ct
Balgeddie Grn
Aboyne Way
Collydean Piper Drive
Pitcairn House (remains)

Balgeddie Way
Road
Netherby Pk
Brent Pl
Dunlin Av
FB
WESTERN AVENUE
3

The Secret Garden
Culdees Ave
Formonthills Road
Holm Sq
Sandray Pk
Harris Pk
Rona

Balgeddie House Hotel
Cardean Way
Errol Gdns
Pitcoudie Roundabout
Crowlin Ave
Eriskay Sq
Tarassay Rd

Balgeddie
Ardoch Park
Pitcoudie
Cumbrae Pk
Bute Pl
Colonsay Sq
Kerrera Pl

Ballingall Drive
Lennox Court
Morven Pk
Argyll Gdns
Oldany Rd
Shuna Sq
Stroma Way
Lismore Ct
Pitcoudie Av

Tweedsmuir Ct
Greenmantle Way
Ballingall Park
Glenmore Ct
Atholl Way
Crescent
Uist Rd
B969
Pitcoudie Primary
Cran

Greenmantle Pl
Cowal
Badalbane Cres
Kinfail Ct
Lochaber Ct
Iona Park
Huntsm

Huntingtow Park
Bradgate Gdns
Cadham Road
Lady Alice Path
Fordel
France Path

nnyknowe
Whinnyhill Plantation
Colinton Ct
Leslie Parks
Juniper Hill
Blanche Path
Aitken
Cadham

Liberton Drive
Braehead Way
Cramond Way
Cedar Drive
Lodge
Rise
Larch Ave
Cornel

Granton Ct
Holyrood Ave
A911
WESTERN
Lodge
Fleming Pl
Aspen Avenue
Larch Ave
Cornel
Beechwood Pl
Water Works

Leslie Bridge
Leslie Mains
Johnstone Path
Somerville Way
Glenrothes Hospital
Pine La
Lane
Beechwood Ave
Beechwood Pk

Hotel
Leslie Rbt
Munro Ct
Jennie Lee La
Docherty Gdns
Elm
Beechwood Ct
Beechwood Drive

Leslie House (Eventide Home)
Forester's Lodge

Lady's Bridge
Picnic Site & Walks
Cow Bridge
LESLIE ROAD

rnhill Ct
Meltrose Ct
Roxburgh
Gifford Ct
Riverside Park
Riverside Park
5
Res

ayton Ct
Ancrum Ct
Lothian Ct
Ednam Dr
South Wood
Almond Path
Alder La
See Town Centre Plan on page 53
Fullerton

edonia
Carfrae Drive
Glenrothes High
Willow
Maple Pl
Cherry Ave
Crescent
Almond Way
Myrtle Ave
Jubilee Gro
Hazel Hill
Rothes Rbt
Fullerton Path
LESLIE

Haddington Cres
Langholm Cres
Lauder Ct
South Parks
Murdoch Pl
Elliot Pl
Moir Pl
Maxwell Pl
South Parks Primary
Morrison Pl
Camel
51
Buchan Path
Napier
Napier Avenue
Munro Pl
Road
North

Index to street names can be found starting on page 99

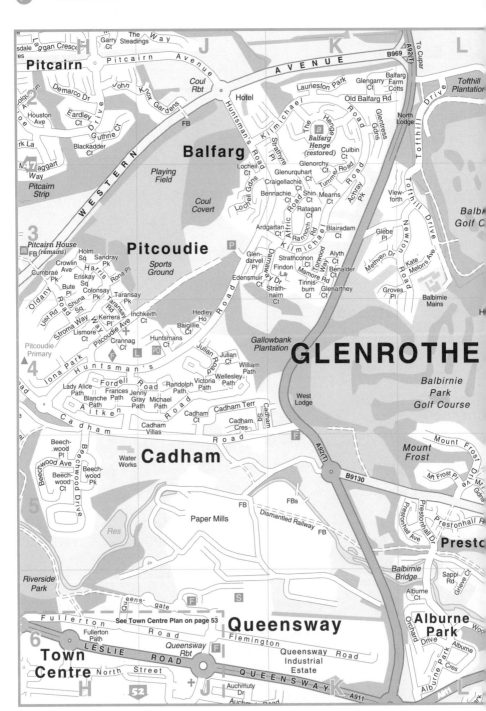

Pitcairn

Balfarg

Pitcoudie

Cadham

GLENROTHE

Balbirnie
Park
Golf Course

Queensway

Town
Centre

Alburne
Park

See Town Centre Plan on page 53

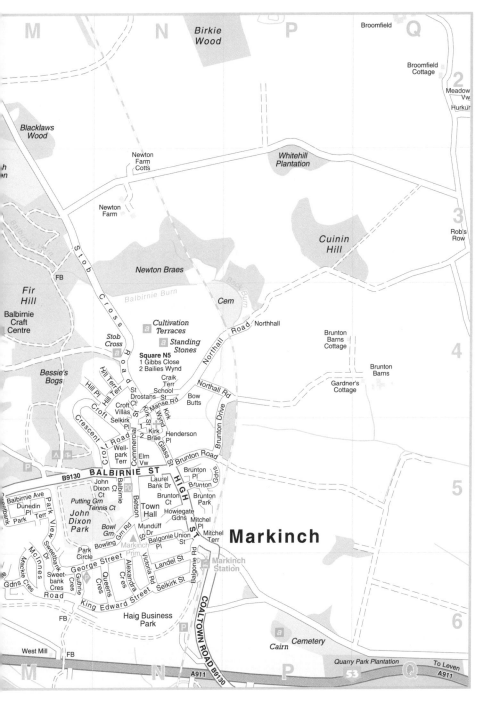

Index to street names can be found starting on page 99

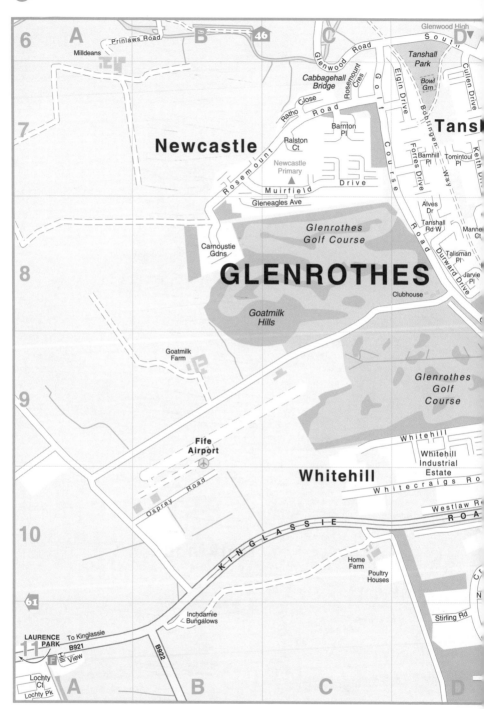

6

A Prinlaws Road **B** 46 **C** Glenwood Road Road South **D**

Milldeans

Glenwood High

Tanshall Park

Cabbagehall Bridge

Rosemount Cres

Golf

Elgin Drive

Bowl Grn

Cullen Drive

Patho Close

Road

7 **Newcastle**

Ralston Ct

Barnton Pl

Boblingen

Forres Drive

Barnhill Pl

Tomintoul Pl

Tans

Keith

Way

Rosemount

Newcastle Primary

Drive

Course

Muirfield

Gleneagles Ave

Alves Dr

Tanshall Rd W

Manne Ct

8 **GLENROTHES**

Glenrothes Golf Course

Carnoustie Gdns

Road

Talisman Pl

Durward Drive

Jarvie Pl

Clubhouse

Goatmilk Hills

Goatmilk Farm

Glenrothes Golf Course

9

Whitehill

Whitehill Industrial Estate

Fife Airport

Whitehill

Whitecraigs Ro

Osprey Road

Westlaw R

ROA

10 KINGLASSIE

Home Farm

Poultry Houses

61

Inchdarnie Bungalows

Stirling Rd

LAURENCE PARK To Kinglassie

B921

B922

11 View

Lochty Ct

A

Lochty Pk

B

C

D

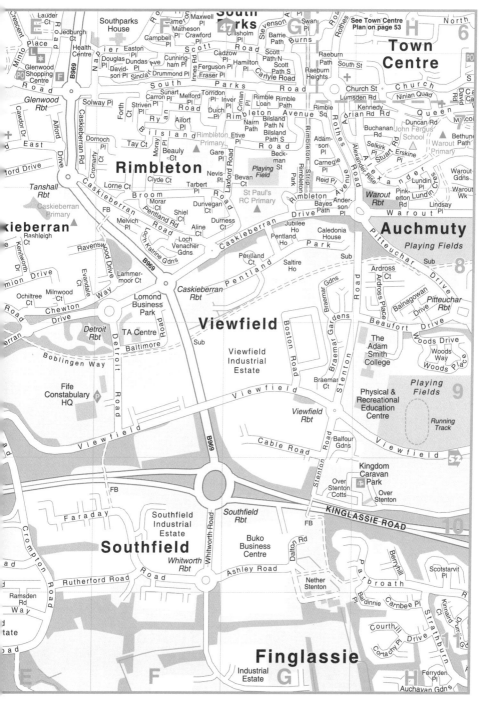

Index to street names can be found starting on page 99

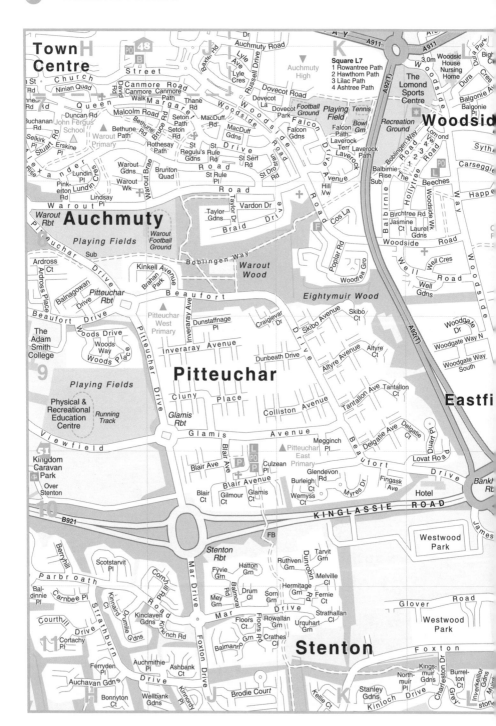

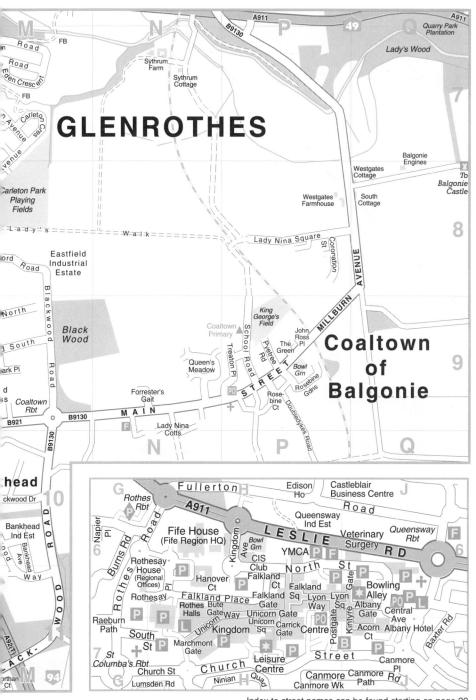

A911

B9130

A911

Quarry Park Plantation

49

Lady's Wood

M

N

P

Q

7

FB

Road

Road

Eden Crescent

FB

Sythrum Farm

Sythrum Cottage

Carleton Ceases

Avenue

Balgonie Engines

To Balgonie Castle

Westgates Cottage

GLENROTHES

Carleton Park Playing Fields

Westgates Farmhouse

South Cottage

8

Lady's Walk

Lady Nina Square

ord Road

Eastfield Industrial Estate

Coronation St

Millburn Avenue

North

Blackwood Road

Black Wood

King George's Field

Coaltown Primary

John Ross Pl

South

Coaltown of Balgonie

ark Pl

Queen's Meadow

School Road

Pyetree Rd

Treaton Pl

The Green

Bowl Grn

9

d

s

Coaltown Rbt

Forrester's Gait

STREET

Rosebine Gdns

B921

B9130

B9130

MAIN

PO

Rosebine Ct

Doubledykes Road

Lady Nina Cotts

N

P

Q

head

ckwood Dr

10

G

Fullerton

Edison Ho

Castleblair Business Centre

J

Rothes Rbt

A911

Road

Bankhead Ind Est

Napier

Rothesay Road

Burns Rd

Fife House (Fife Region HQ)

LESLIE

Queensway Ind Est

Veterinary Surgery

Queensway Rbt

F

6

Kingdom Ave

Bowl Grn

RD

6

od

Bankhead Ave

ROAD

Way

Rothesay House (Regional Offices)

Hanover Ct

CIS Club

Falkland

North

St

YMCA

P

F

Bowling Alley

A921(T)

WOOD

Rothesay Pl

Falkland Place

Falkland Ct

Falkland Sq

Lyon Way

Lyon Sq

Albany Gate

Central Ave

Raeburn Path

Rothes Halls

Bute Gate

Unicorn Way

Unicorn Gate

Carrick Gate

PO

Acorn Ct

Albany Hotel

Baxter Rd

BLACK-

South St

Kingdom Sq

Centre

Postgate

Kintyre

PO

L

7

St Columba's Rbt

Marchmont Gate

Leisure Centre

Street

Canmore Pl

M

94

rthan

Church St

Church

Canmore

Canmore Rd

Path

J

G

Lumsden Rd

Ninian

Qua

Canmore Wk

H

Index to street names can be found starting on page 99

Sat Feb 8 Sc Start | D = Do

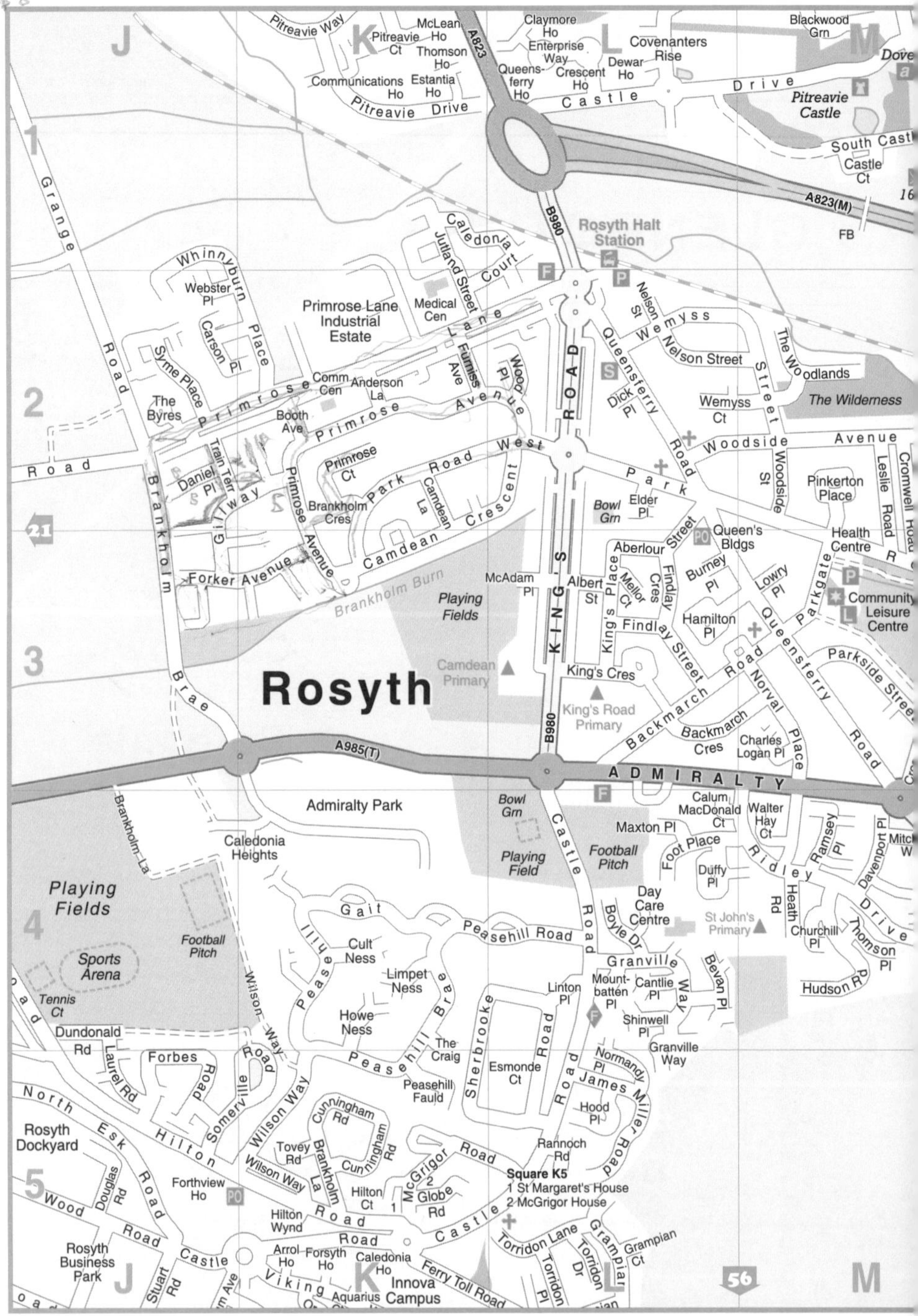
J
K
L
M
1
2
3
4
5
Pitreavie Way
Pitreavie Ct
McLean Ho
Thomson Ho
Communications Ho
Estantia Ho
Pitreavie Drive
A823
Claymore Ho
Enterprise Way
Queensferry Ho
Crescent Ho
Dewar Ho
Covenanters Rise
Castle Drive
Blackwood Grn
Pitreavie Castle
South Castle
Castle Ct
A823(M)
FB
Grange Road
B980
Rosyth Halt Station
Caledonia Court
Jutland Street
Whinnyburn Place
Webster Pl
Carson Pl
Syme Place
Primrose Lane Industrial Estate
Medical Cen
Primrose Lane
Furniss Ave
Wood Pl
Comm Cen
Anderson La
The Byres
Booth Ave
Primrose Avenue
Road
Train Terr
Daniel Pl
Gillway
Primrose Ct
Park Road West
Camdean La
Camdean Crescent
Brankholm Cres
Primrose Avenue
Forker Avenue
Brankholm Brae
Brankholm Burn
McAdam Pl
Playing Fields
Camdean Primary
Rosyth
KING'S ROAD
Nelson St
Wemyss
Nelson Street
Queensferry Road
Dick Pl
Street
The Woodlands
The Wilderness
Wemyss Ct
Woodside Avenue
Woodside St
Pinkerton Place
Leslie Road
Cromwell Road
Park
Bowl Grn
Elder Pl
Aberlour Street
PO
Queen's Bldgs
Health Centre
Albert St
King's Place
Mellor Ct
Findlay Cres
Burney Pl
Lowry Pl
Parkgate
Community Leisure Centre
Hamilton Pl
Findlay Street
Queensferry Road
Parkside Street
King's Cres
King's Road Primary
Backmarch Road
Norval Place
Backmarch Cres
Charles Logan Pl
A985(T)
ADMIRALTY
Admiralty Park
Brankholm La
Caledonia Heights
Bowl Grn
Playing Field
Castle Road
Football Pitch
Calum MacDonald Ct
Walter Hay Ct
Maxton Pl
Foot Place
Ramsey Pl
Davenport Pl
Duffy Pl
Ridley Drive
Heath Rd
Day Care Centre
St John's Primary
Churchill Pl
Thomson Pl
Hudson Rd
Playing Fields
Sports Arena
Football Pitch
Tennis Ct
Gait
Peasehill Road
Cult Ness
Limpet Ness
Howe Ness
Peasehill Brae
Boyle Dr
Granville Way
Bevan Pl
Linton Pl
Mountbatten Pl
Cantlie Pl
Shinwell Pl
Granville Way
Wilson Way
Dundonald Rd
Laurel Rd
Forbes Road
Somerville Road
The Craig
Peasehill Fauld
Sherbrooke Road
Esmonde Ct
Normandy Pl
James Miller Road
Hood Pl
North Esk Road
Hilton Road
Rosyth Dockyard
Cunningham Rd
Tovey Rd
Brankholm La
Wilson Way
McGrigor Road
Globe Rd
Hilton Ct
Rannoch Rd
Square K5
1 St Margaret's House
2 McGrigor House
Wood Road
Douglas Rd
Forthview Ho
Hilton Wynd
Castle Road
Castle
Torridon Lane
Torridon Dr
Grampian Ct
Rosyth Business Park
Stuart Rd
Arrol Ho
Forsyth Ho
Caledonia Ho
Viking Way
Aquarius
Innova Campus
Ferry Toll Road
Torridon Pl
21
56

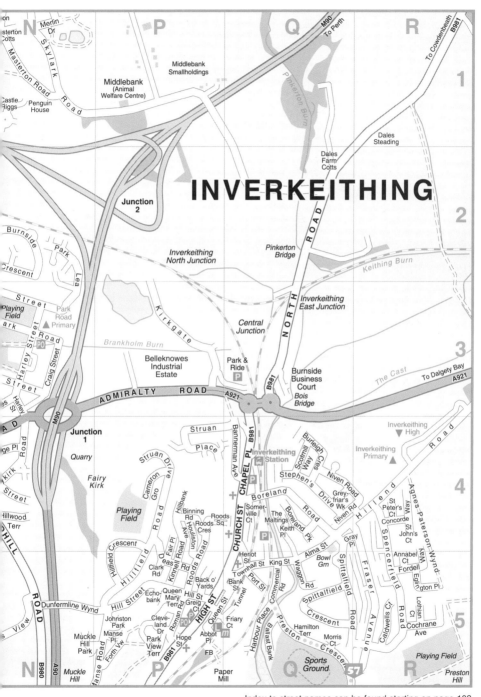

INVERKEITHING

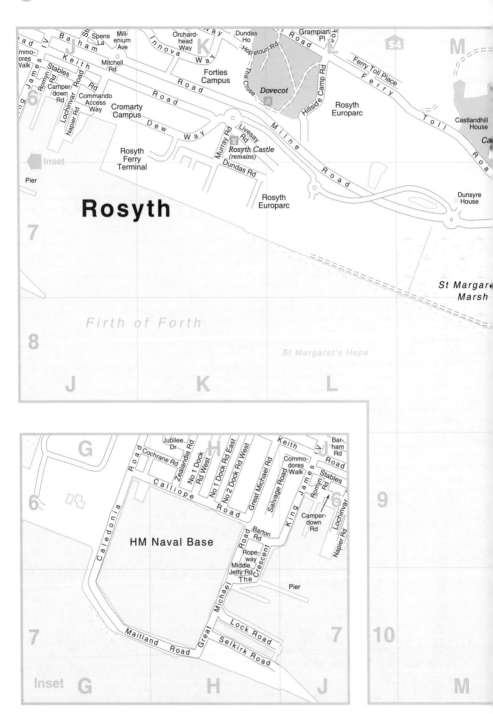

Rosyth

Firth of Forth

St Margaret's Hope

HM Naval Base

Inset

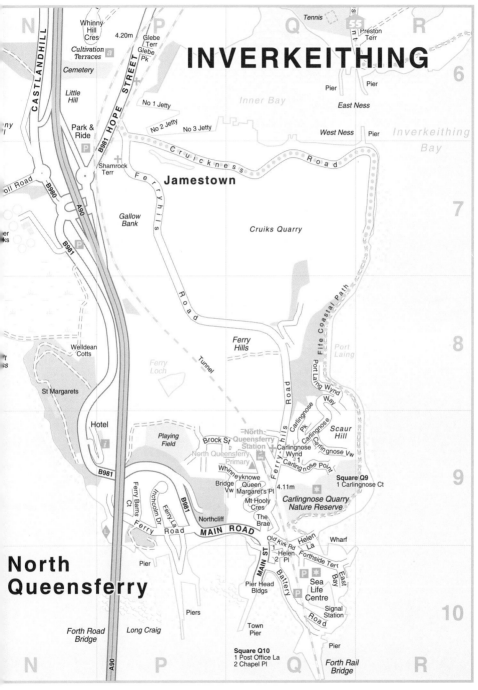

INVERKEITHING

N

Whinny Hill Cres
4.20m
Glebe Terr
Glebe Pk
Cultivation Terraces
Cemetery
Little Hill

P

Tennis

Q

Preston Terr

R

6

Pier
Pier
East Ness

Inner Bay

No 1 Jetty

West Ness
Pier

Inverkeithing Bay

CASTLANDHILL
HOPE STREET
B981

Park & Ride
No 2 Jetty
No 3 Jetty

ny

oll Road

B980

Shamrock Terr

Cruickness Road

A90

Ferryhills

Jamestown

Gallow Bank

Cruiks Quarry

7

B981

Road

ny

er
ks

Ferry Hills

Fife Coastal Path

Port Laing

8

Welldean Cotts

St Margarets

Ferry Loch

Tunnel

Road

Port Laing Wynd
Way

t
ss

Hotel

Playing Field

Brock St

North Queensferry Station

North Queensferry Primary

Carlingnose Pk

Carlingnose Wynd

Carlingnose Vw

Scaur Hill

B981

Ferry Barns Ct
Inchcolm Dr
Ferry La

Whinneyknowe
Bridge Vw
Queen Margaret's Pl
Mt Hooly Cres

1
Carlingnose Point

Square Q9
1 Carlingnose Ct

9

Ferry Hills

4.11m

Carlingnose Quarry Nature Reserve

North Queensferry

Northcliff

The Brae

MAIN ROAD

Old Kirk Rd
Helen La
Helen Pl
1
2
Forthside Terr

Wharf

East Bay

Pier

MAIN ST

Battery

Pier Head Bldgs

Sea Life Centre

Signal Station

10

Piers

Forth Road Bridge
Long Craig

Town Pier

Road

Square Q10
1 Post Office La
2 Chapel Pl

Pier

Forth Rail Bridge

A90

N

P

Q

R

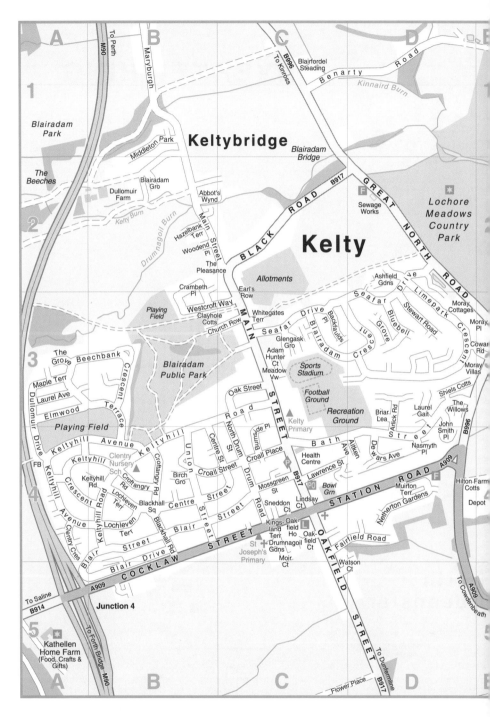

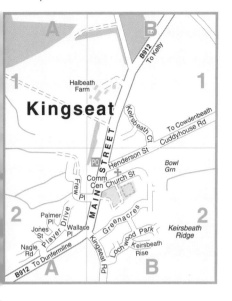

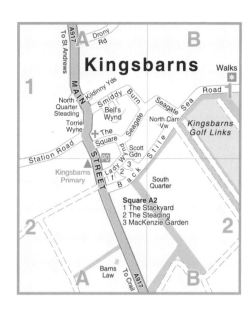

Index to Kelty

Abbot's Wynd	B2
Adam Hunter Court	C3
Aitken Avenue	D4
Arlick Road	D3
Ashfield Gardens	D2
Backfaulds Place	C3
Bath Street	C4
Beechbank Crescent	B3
Benarty Road	C1
Birch Grove	B4
Black Road	C2
Blackhall Road	B4
Blackhall Square	B4
Blair Drive	B5
Blair Street	B4
Blairadam Crescent	C3
Blairadam Grove	B2
Blairfordel Steading	C1
Bluebell Grove	D3
Briar Lea	D3
Burnside Place	C4
Centre Street	B4
Church Row	C3
Clayhole Cottages	B3
Clentry Crescent	A4
Cocklaw Street	B5
Cowan Road	D3
Crambeth Place	B3
Croall Place	C4
Croall Street	B4
Croftangry Road	B4

Dewars Avenue	D4
Drum Road	C4
Drumnagoil Gardens	C4
Dullomuir Drive	A3
Earl's Row	C2
Elmwood Terrace	A3
Fairfield Road	D4
Flower Place	C5
Glengask Grove	C3
Great North Road	D2
Grove, The	A3
Hazelbank Terrace	B2
Hilton Farm	D4
Cottages	
John Smith Place	D4
Keltyhill Avenue	A4
Keltyhill Crescent	A4
Keltyhill Road	B4
Kingsland Terrace	C4
Laurel Avenue	A3
Laurel Gait	D3
Lawrence Street	C4
Limepark Crescent	D3
Lindsay Court	C4
Lochleven Terrace	B4
Main Street	C3
Maple Terrace	A3
Maryburgh	B1
Meadow View	C3
Middleton Park	B1
Moir Court	C4
Moray Cottages	D3
Moray Place	D3

Moray Villas	D3
Mossgreen Street	C4
Muirton Terrace	D4
Nasmyth Place	D4
Netherton Gardens	D4
North Drum Street	C3
Oak Street	C3
Oakfield Court	C4
Oakfield House	C4
Oakfield Street	C5
Pleasance, The	B2
Seafar Drive	C3, D3
Shiels Cottages	D3
Sneddon Court	C4
Station Road	D4
Stewart Road	D3
Union Street	B4
Watson Court	C5
Westcroft Way	B3
Whitegates Terrace	C3
Willows, The	D3
Woodend Place	B2

Index to Kingsbarns

Back Stile	A2
Bell's Wynd	A1
Drony Road	A1
Kildinny Yards	A1
Lady Wynd	A2
MacKenzie Garden (3)	A2

Main Street	A1
North Carr View	B1
North Quarter Steading	A1
Scott Garden	A1
Sea Road	B1
Seagate	B1
Smiddy Burn	A1
Square, The	A1
Stackyard, The (1)	A2
Station Road	A1
Steading, The (2)	A2
Torrie Wyne	A1

Index to Kingseat

Church Street	B2
Cuddyhouse Road	B1
Frew Place	A2
Greenacres	B2
Henderson Street	B2
Jones Street	A2
Keirsbeath Court	B1
Keirsbeath Rise	B2
Kingseat Road	B2
Lochwood Park	B2
Main Street	B2
Nagle Road	A2
Palmer Place	A2
Player Drive	A2
Wallace Place	A2

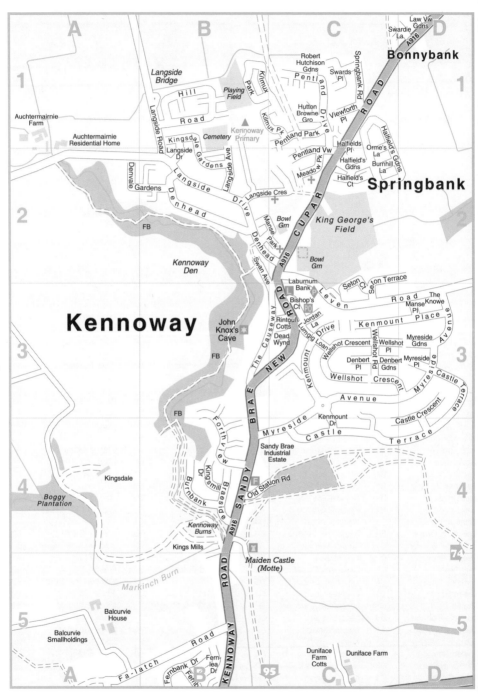

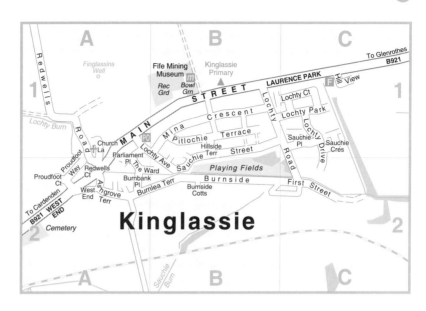

Kinglassie

Index to Kennoway

Bishop's Court	C3
Braeside	B4
Burnbank	B4
Burnhill Lane	C2
Castle Crescent	D3
Castle Terrace	C4
Causeway, The	B3
Cupar Road	C2
Dead Wynd	C3
Denbert Gardens	C3
Denbert Place	C3
Denhead	B2
Denvale Gardens	A2
Duniface Farm Cottages	C5
Fa-latch Road	B5
Fernlea Drive	B5
Forthview	B4
Halfield's Court	C2
Halfield's Gardens	C2
Halfields Place	C1
Hill Road	B1
Hutton Browne Grove	C1
Jordan Lane	C3
Kenmount Drive	C3
Kenmount Place	C3
Kennoway Road	B5
Kilmux Park	B1
Kingsdale Gardens	B1
Kingsmill Drive	B4
Knowe, The	D3
Laburnum Bank	C2

Langside Avenue	B2
Langside Crescent	B2
Langside Drive	B2
Langside Road	B1
Law View Gardens	D1
Leven Road	C3
Lumgig Loan	C3
Manse Park	C2
Manse Place	D3
Meadow Park	C2
Myreside Avenue	C3
Myreside Gardens	D3
Myreside Place	D3
New Road	C3
Old Station Road	B4
Orme's Lane	C1
Pentland Drive	C1
Pentland Park	C1
Pentland View	C2
Rintoul Cottages	C3
Robert Hutchison Gardens	C1
Sandy Brae	B4
Seton Court	C3
Seton Terrace	C3
Springbank Road	C1
Swan Avenue	B2
Swardie Lane	D1
Swards Place	C1
Viewforth Place	C1
Wellshot Crescent	C3
Wellshot Place	C3
Wellshot Road	C3

Index to Kinglassie

Ashgrove Terrace	A2
Burnbank Place	A2
Burnlea Terrace	A2
Burnside Cottages	B2
Burnside	B2
Church Lane	A1
First Street	C2
Hill View	C1
Hillside Terrace	B1
Laurence Park	B1
Lochty Avenue	A1
Lochty Court	C1
Lochty Drive	C1
Lochty Park	C1
Lochty Road	B1
Main Street	A1
Mina Crescent	B1
Parliament Place	A1
Pitlochie Terrace	B1
Proudfoot Court	A2
Proudfoot Way	A2
Redwells Court	A2
Redwells Road	A1
Sauchie Crescent	C2
Sauchie Place	C1
Sauchie Street	B2
Ward, The	A2
West End	A2

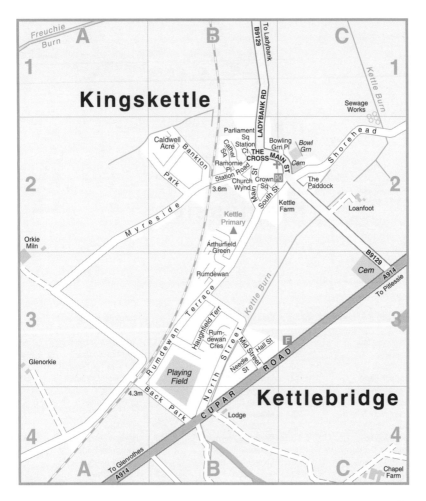

Index to Kingskettle & Kettlebridge

Arthurfield Green	B2	Paddock, The	C2
Back Park	B4	Parliament Square	B2
Bankton Park	B2	Ramornie Place	B2
Bowling Green Place	C2	Rumdewan Crescent	B3
Caldwell Acre	B2	Rumdewan Terrace	B3
Cathel Square	B2	Rumdewan	B3
Church Wynd	B2	Shorehead	C2
Cross, The	B2	South Street	B2
Crown Square	B2	Station Court	B2
Cupar Road	B4	Station Road	B2
Hall Street	B3		
Haughfield Terrace	B3		
Ladybank Road	B2		
Main Street	B2		
Mid Street	B3		
Myreside	A2		
Needle Street	B3		
North Street	B3		

Index to Kinghorn & Pettycur

Abden Avenue	C5	Boswell Drive	C5
Abden Court	C5	Bruce Street	C5
Abden Place	C5	Bruce Terrace	C5
Alexander III Street	B7	Burnside Avenue	B5
Baliol Street	B6	Burntisland Road	A7
Barclay Road	B5	Burt Avenue	B5
Barton Buildings	C5	Canmore Street	B6
Birrel's Wynd (6)	C5	Carlin Craig	B7
		Carlin Crescent	B7
		Castle Wynd (3)	B5
		Castlerig	B6
		Church Walk	C5
		Croft An Righ	C4
		Cuinzie Neuk (4)	B5
		Darney Terrace	B6
		David I Street	B6
		Doo-Dells Lane	B6
		Eastgate	B5
		Glamis Road	B5
		Glamis Terrace	B5
		Glebe Place	B5

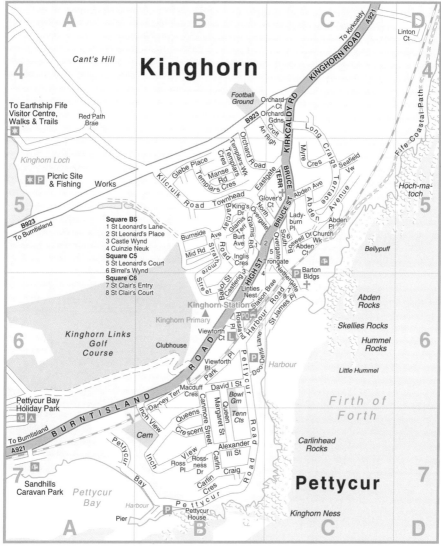

Glover's Court	C5	Manse Road	B5	Queens Crescent	B7	Seafield View	C5
Harbour Road	B6	Mid Road	B5	Red Path Brae	A4	South Overgate	C5
High Street	B6	Myre Crescent	C5	Ross Place	B7	Station Brae	B6
Inch View	B7	Nethergate	C6	Rossland Place	B6	Strathmore Street	B5
Inglis Crescent	B5	North Overgate	B5	Rossness Drive	B7	Templars Crescent	B5
Kilcruik Road	B5	Orchard Court	C4	St Clair's Court (8)	C6	Templars Walk	B5
Kinghorn Road	C4	Orchard Gardens	C4	St Clair's Entry (7)	C6	Townhead	B5
King's Drive	B5	Orchard Road	B5	St James Place	C6	Trongate	C5
Kirkcaldy Road	C5	Park Place	B6	St Leonard's		Viewforth Court	B6
Ladyburn Place	C5	Pettycur Bay	A7	Court (5)	C5	Viewforth Place	B6
Linties Nest	B6	Pettycur House	B7	St Leonard's			
Linton Court	D4	Pettycur Road	B6	Lane (1)	B5		
Long Craigs Terrace	C4	Queen Margaret	B6	St Leonard's			
MacDuff Crescent	B6	Street		Place (2)	B5		

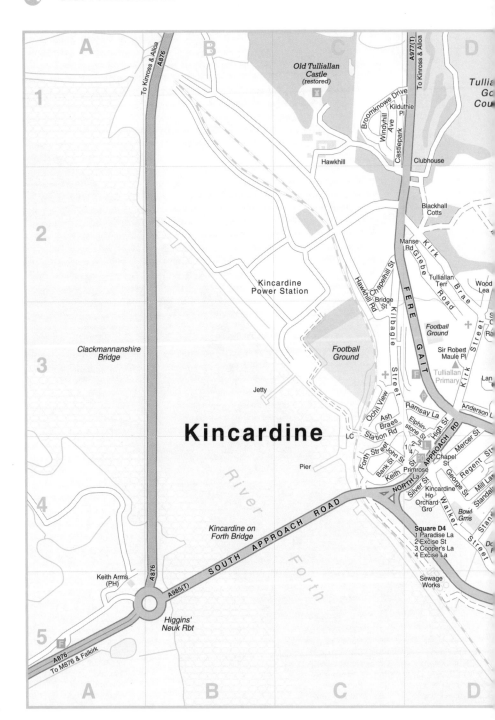

Old Tulliallan
Castle
(restored)

To Kinross & Alloa
A876

A977(T)
To Kinross & Alloa

Tullia
Go
Cou

Broomknowe Drive

Windyhill Ave

Kilduthie Pl

Castlepark

Clubhouse

Hawkhill

Blackhall
Cotts

Manse
Rd

Kirk

Glebe

Tulliallan
Terr

Wood
Lea

Kincardine
Power Station

Hawkhill Rd

Chapelhill St

Bridge
St

FERE GAIT

Kilbagie Street

Football
Ground

Football
Ground

Sir Robert
Maule Pl

Kirk Street

Ra

Tulliallan
Primary

Lan

Clackmannanshire
Bridge

Jetty

Ochil View

Ash
Braes

Station Rd

Ramsay La

Elphin-
stone St

High St

Anderson L

APPROACH RD

Mercer St

Regent St

Kincardine

LC

Forth Street

Bank St

John St

Keith

1 2·3

Primrose
La

Chapel
St

George St

Mill La

Standal

Silver St

NORTH

Kincardine
Ho

Bowl
Grns

Orchard
Gro

Square D4
1 Paradise La
2 Excise St
3 Cooper's La
4 Excise La

Walker Street

Stan

River

Forth

Kincardine on
Forth Bridge

SOUTH APPROACH ROAD

Do

Sewage
Works

Keith Arms
(PH)

A876

A985(T)

Higgins'
Neuk Rbt

A876
To M876 & Falkirk

Pier

Index to Kincardine

Anderson Lane	D3
Ash Braes	C3
Bank Street	C4
Blackhall Cottages	D2
Bridge Street	C2
Broomknowe Drive	C1
Burn Brae Park	E3
Castlepark	C1
Chapel Street	D4
Chapelhill Street	C2
Cooper's Lane (3)	D4
Dewar Avenue	D3
Donaldson Court	D4
Elphinstone Street	D3
Excise Lane (4)	D4
Excise Street (2)	D4
Fere Gait	D2
Forth Street	C4
Forth View	E4
George Street	D4
Glebe Road	D2
Hawkhill Road	C2
High Street	D3
James Wylie Place	E3
John Street	C4
Keith Street	C4
Kellywood Crescent	E4
Kilbagie Street	C3
Kilduthie Place	C1
Kincardine House	D4
Kirk Brae	D2
Kirk Street	D3
Lansdowne Crescent	D3
Manse Road	D2
Mercer Street	D4
Middle Drive	D2
Mill Lane	D4
North Approach Road	C4
Ochil View	C3
Orchard Grove	D4
Osborne Drive	E3
Paradise Lane (1)	D4
Primrose Lane	D4
Priory Square	E4
Ramsay Court	D3
Ramsay Lane	D3
Regent Street	D4
Riverside Terrace	D4
Roanhead Terrace	D3
Rosebank Gardens	D4
Silver Street	D4
Sir Robert Maule Place	D3
Sivewright Court	D3
South Approach Road	B5
Standalane	D4
Station Road	C3
Tarbert Terrace	E4
Toll Road	E4
Tulliallan Terrace	D2
Walker Street	D4
Windyhill Avenue	C1
Wood Lea	D2

E

1

Castle
Police
ge

Tulliallan
Wood

2

3

Pk

ROAD
riory Sq
To Dunfermline
A977
d
Tarbert
Terr
Cem

Longannet
Rbt

A985(T)
To Dunfermline

4

he Sycamores
nch House

5

E

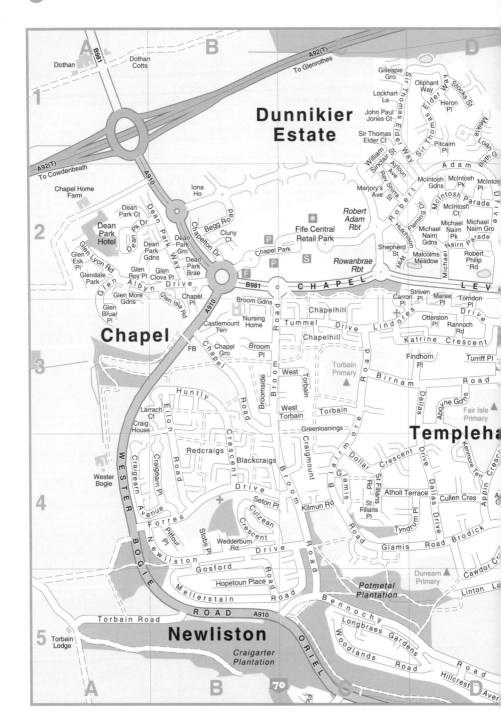

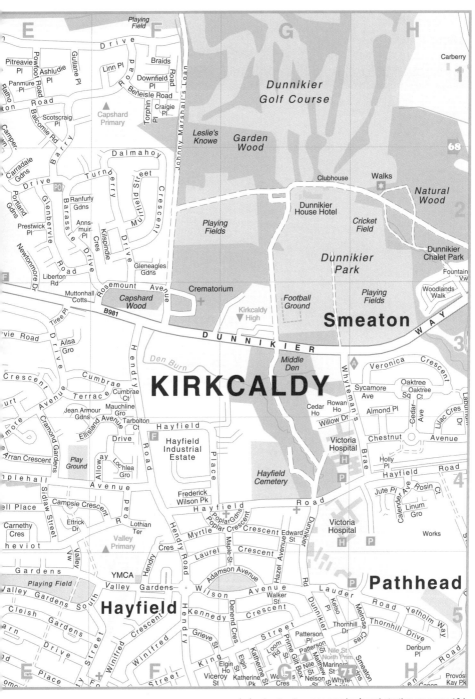

Index to street names can be found starting on page 104

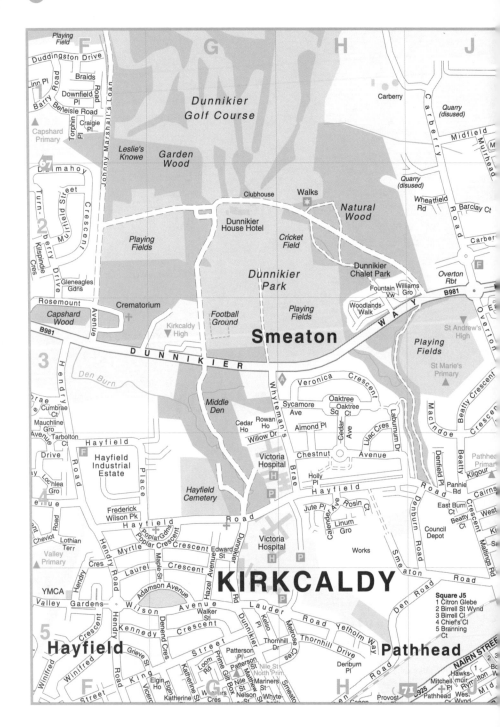

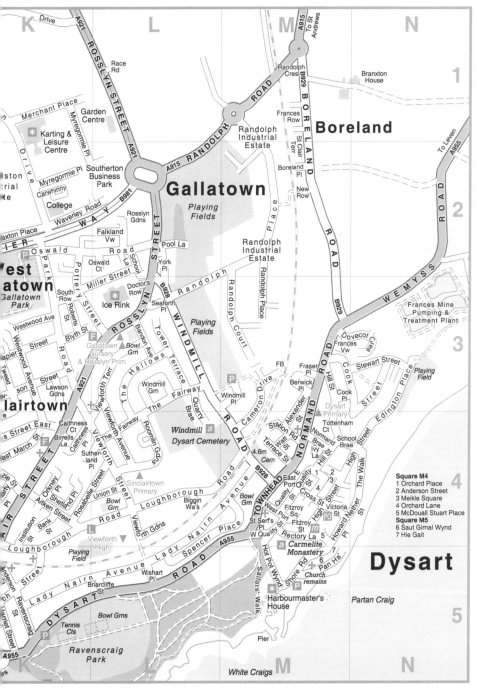

Index to street names can be found starting on page 104

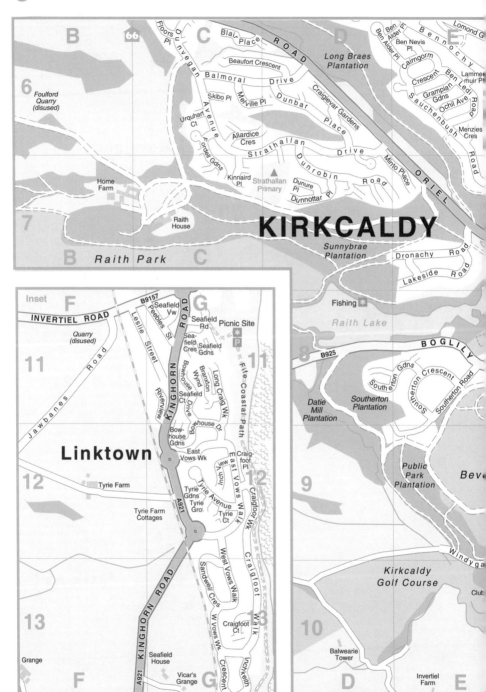

KIRKCALDY

Linktown

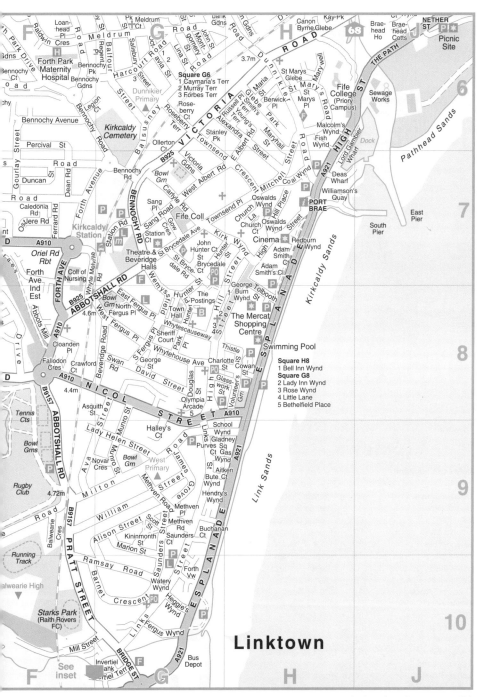

Linktown

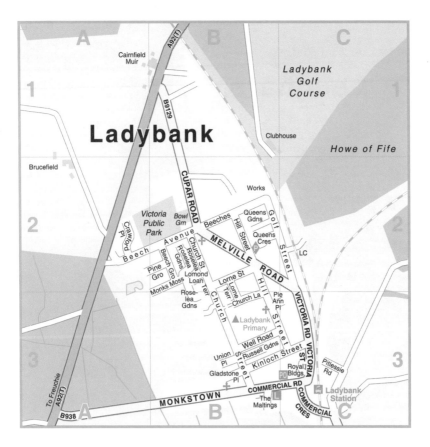

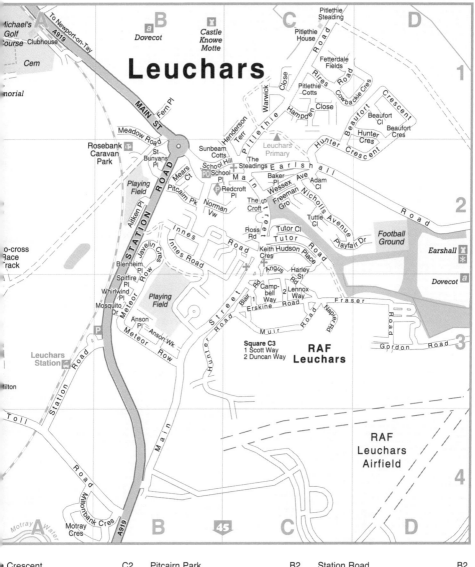

Leuchars

Square C3
1 Scott Way
2 Duncan Way

RAF Leuchars

RAF Leuchars Airfield

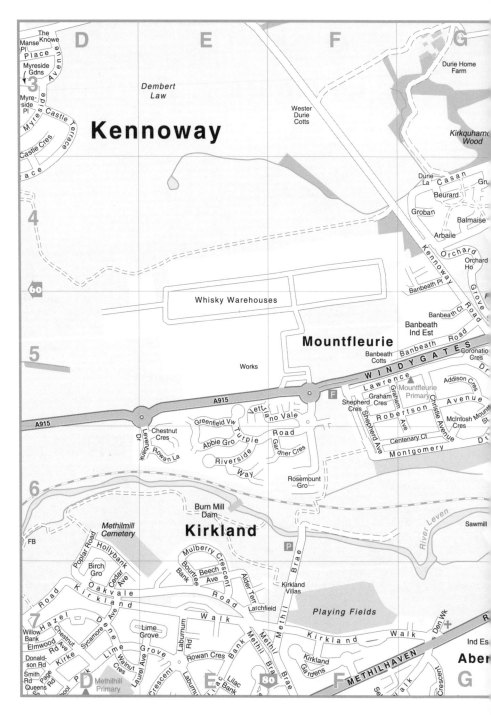

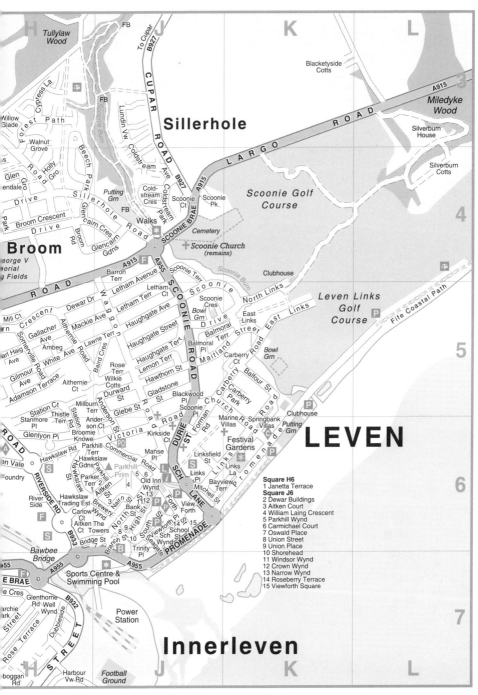

Square H6
1 Janetta Terrace
Square J6
2 Dewar Buildings
3 Aitken Court
4 William Laing Crescent
5 Parkhill Wynd
6 Carmichael Court
7 Oswald Place
8 Union Street
9 Union Place
10 Shorehead
11 Windsor Wynd
12 Crown Wynd
13 Narrow Wynd
14 Roseberry Terrace
15 Viewforth Square

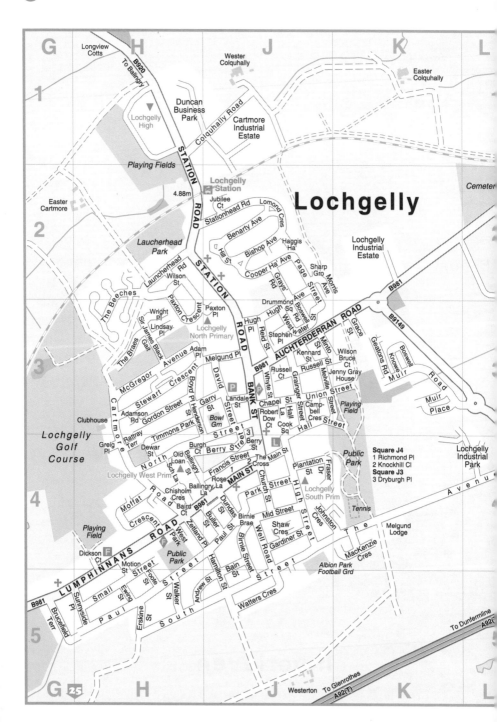

Lochgelly

Square J4
1 Richmond Pl
2 Knockhill Cl
Square J3
3 Dryburgh Pl

ex to Lochgelly

am Place	H3	Hamilton Street	J4	Sunnyside Place	H5
amson Road	H3	Henderson Street	H3	Timmons Park	H3
drew Street	H5	High Street	J4	Union Street	J3
chterderran Road	J3	Hill Street	J2	Walker Street	H5
nue, The	K4	Hugh Avenue	J3	Watters Crescent	J5
n Street	J4	Hugh Place	J3	Well Road	J4
rd Court	H4	Jenny Gray House	K3	West Park	H4
lingry Lane	H4	Johnston Crescent	J4	Westwater Street	J3
ingry Street	H4	Jubilee Court	J2	Whyte Street	J3
k Street	J3	Kennard Street	J3	Wilson Bruce Court	K3
eches, The	H2	Knockhill Close (2)	J4	Wilson Street	H2
arty Avenue	J2	Landale Street	J3	Wright Place	H3
ry Street	J4	Launcherhead Road	H2	Zetland Place	H4
ie Brae	J4	Lindsay Place	H3		
ie Street	J4	Lomond Crescent	J2		
hop Avenue	J2	Longview Cottages	H1		
swell Knowe	K3	Lumphinnans Road	H4		
swell Road	J3	McGregor Avenue	H3		
rd Place	H3	MacKenzie Crescent	K4		
es, The	H3	Main Street	J4		
cefield Terrace	G5	Melgund Place	J3		
ler Street	J4	Melville Street	J3		
gh Court	H4	Mid Street	J4		
npbell Crescent	J3	Minto Street	J3		
tmore Road	H4	Moffat Crescent	H4		
apel Street	J3	Morris Avenue	J2		
sholm Crescent	H4	Motion Street	H4		
urch Street	J4	Muir Place	K3		
quhally Road	J1	Muir Road	K3		
ok Square	J3	North Street	H4		
pper Ha' Avenue	J2	Old Loan	H4		
ss, The	J4	Page Street	J2		
rid Street	J3	Park Street	J4		
var Street	H4	Paul Street	H5, J4		
kson Court	H4	Paxton Crescent	H3		
mmond Square	J3	Paxton Place	J3		
burgh Place (3)	J3	Plantation Street	J4		
ndas Street	J4	Rattray Terrace	H4		
kine Street	H5	Reid Street	J3		
ng Street	H5	Richmond Place (1)	J4		
te Street	H5	Robert Dow Court	J3		
ncis Street	J4	Rose Lane	J4		
ser Drive	J4	Russell Court	J3		
rdiner Street	J4	Russell Street	J3		
ry Street	J3	School Lane	H4		
atons Road	K3	Sharp Grove	J2		
don Street	H3	Shaw Crescent	J4		
ce Street	K3	Sir James Black Gait	H3		
inger Street	J3	Small Street	H5		
ys' Road	J2	South Street	J5		
ig Place	H4	Station Road	H1, H2		
gis Ha'	J2	Stationhead Road	J2		
Lane	J3	Stephen Place	J3		
Street	J3	Stewart Crescent	H3		

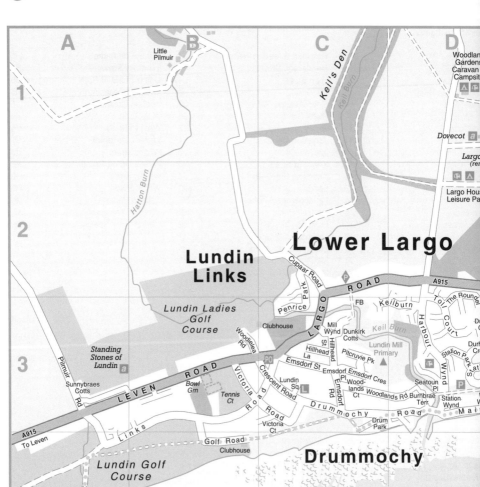

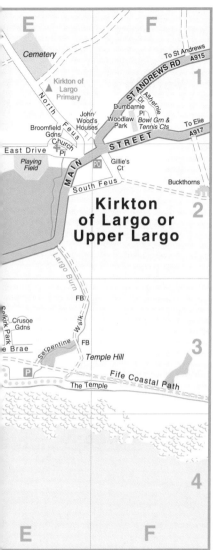

Index to Largo

Aithernie Drive	F1	St Andrews Road	F1
Bourtree Brae	E3	Seatoun Place	D3
Broomfield Gardens	E1	Selkirk Park	E3
Burnbrae Terrace	D3	Serpentine Walk	E3
Church Place	E2	South Feus	E2
Crescent Road	C3	Station Park	D3
Crusoe Gardens	E3	Station Wynd	D3
Cupar Road	C2	Sunnybraes Cottages	A3
Donaldson's Court	D3	Temple, The	E3
Drum Park	C3	Toll Court	D2
Drummochy Road	C3	Victoria Court	C3
Dumbarnie Place	F1	Victoria Road	B3
Dunkirk Cottages	C3	Well Wynd	D3
Durham Crescent	D3	Woodielea Road	B3
Durham Gardens	D3	Woodlands Court	C3
Durham Terrace	D3	Woodlands Road	C3
Durham Wynd	D3	Woodlaw Park	F1
East Drive	E2		
Emsdorf Crescent	C3		
Emsdorf Place	C3		
Emsdorf Road	C3		
Emsdorf Street	C3		
Gillies' Court	F2		
Golf Road	B3		
Harbour Wynd	D3		
Hillhead Lane	C3		
Hillhead Street	C3		
John Wood's Houses	E1		
Keilburn	D3		
Largo Road	C3		
Leven Road	A3		
Links Road	A4		
Lundin Square	C3		
Main Street	D3		
(Lower Largo)			
Main Street	E2		
(Upper Largo)			
Mill Wynd	C3		
North Feus	E1		
Penrice Park	C3		
Pilmuir Road	A3		
Pitcruvie Park	C3		
Roundel, The	D3		

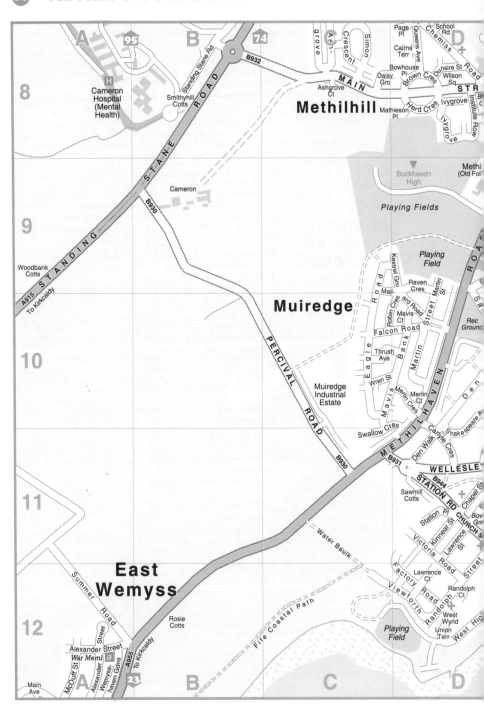

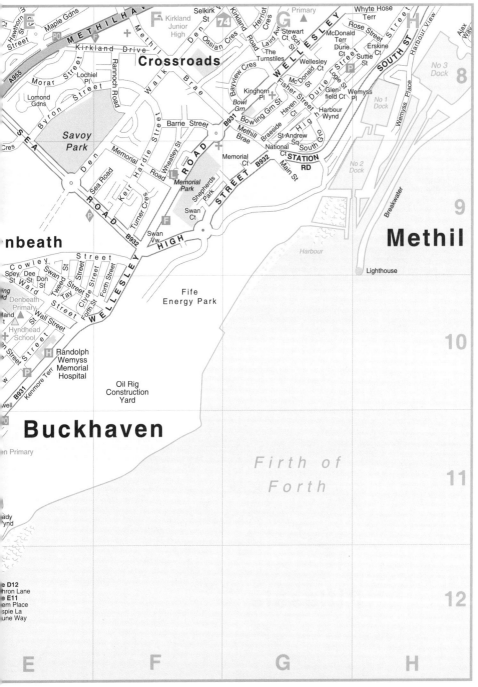

Crossroads

Methil

nbeath

Buckhaven

Firth of
Forth

Kirkland Junior High

Selkirk St

Primary

Whyte Hose Terr

Rose Street

Maple Gdns

Hawthorn Street

Street

Kirkland Drive

Den

Ossian Cres

Kirkland Road

Heriot Cres

Laird Av

Stewart Ct

Sch

Wellesley

McDonald Terr

Durie

Erskine Ct

Suttie St

SOUTH ST

Harbour View

Ajax Way

No 3 Dock

Lochiel Pl

Rannoch Road

The Turnstiles

Wellesley Ct

McDonald St

Footie St

Fogie St

8

Morar Street

Bayview Cres

Fisher Street

Durie St

Glen-field Ct

Wemyss Pl

Wemyss Place

Lomond Gdns

Byron Street

Kinghorn Pl

Bowl Grn

Bowling Grn St

Haven Ct

Harbour Wynd

No 1 Dock

Crescent

SEA

Savoy Park

Barrie Street

B931

Methil Brae

Braeside

High

St Andrew Sq South

National Ct

B932

No 2 Dock

9

Hardie Street

Wheatley St

Memorial Road

Memorial Park

Shepherds Park

Memorial Ct

Main St

STATION RD

Breakwater

Sea Road

Kelir

Turner Cres

Swan Ct

HIGH STREET

Harbour

Lighthouse

Swan Vw

ROAD

B932

Cowley Street

Swan St

Don St

Street

Fife Energy Park

Spey St

Dee St

Tweed Street

Tay Street

Forth Street

Ward

Clyde Street

Forth St

WELLESLEY

Denbeath Primary

Wall Street

Street

10

Hyndhead School

Randolph Wemyss Memorial Hospital

Kenmore Terr

Oil Rig Construction Yard

B931

well

Primary

ady ynd

11

e D12
hron Lane
e E11
em Place
spie La
une Way

12

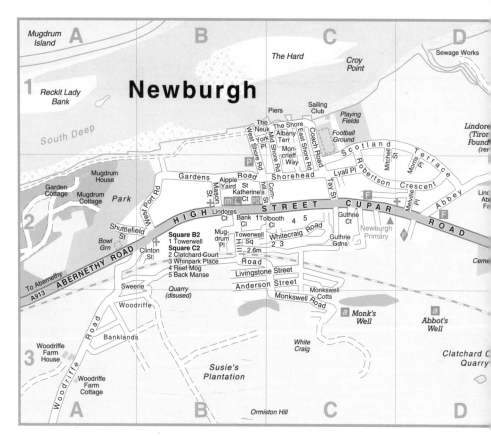

Newburgh

Mugdrum
Island

Reckit Lady
Bank

South Deep

The Hard

Croy
Point

Sewage Works

Piers

Sailing
Club

Playing
Fields

Lindore
(Tiror
Found
(re

The Shore
The Neuk
West York
Albany
Terr
Mid Shore Rd
East Shore Rd
Mon-
crieff
Way

Coach Road

Scotland
Mitchell St
Morris St

Terrace

Mugdrum
House

Gardens

Aipple
Yaird

St
Katherine's
Ct

Road

Shorehead

Lyall Pl

Robertson

Crescent

Abbey

Lind
Ab
Fa

Garden
Cottage
Mugdrum
Cottage

Park

West Port Rd

Mason
St

M L

PO

Com.

Tay St

HIGH

STREET

CUPAR

ROAD

F

Melville
Pl

Lindores
St

Bank
Cl

Tolbooth
Cl

4

5

Guthrie
Ct

Newburgh
Primary

Ceme

Shuttlefield
St

Bowl
Grn

Clinton
St

Square B2
1 Towerwell
Square C2
2 Clatchard Court
3 Whinpark Place
4 Reef Mog
5 Back Manse

Mug-
drum
Pl

Towerwell
Sq

2.6m

Whitecraig

2 3

Road

Guthrie
Gdns

F

Sweerie

Quarry
(disused)

Livingstone Street

Anderson   Street

Monkswell Road

Monkswell
Cotts

Monk's
Well

a

Abbot's
Well

a

Woodriffe

Banklands

White
Craig

Clatchard C
Quarry

Woodriffe
Farm
House

Woodriffe
Road

ABERNETHY ROAD

To Abernethy
A913

Woodriffe
Farm
Cottage

Susie's
Plantation

Ormiston Hill

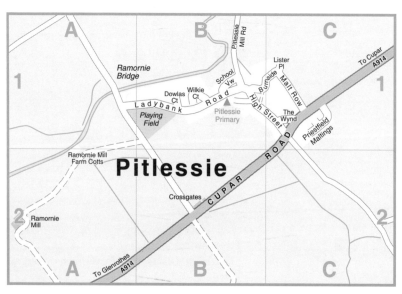

Pitlessie

Ramornie
Bridge

Pitlessie
Mill Rd

Lister
Pl

To Cupar
A914

Dowlas
Ct

Wilkie
Ct

School
Vw

Burnside

Mall Row

Ladybank   Road

Playing
Field

Pitlessie
Primary

High Street

The
Wynd

Priestfield
Maltings

Ramornie Mill
Farm Cotts

CUPAR

ROAD

Crossgates

Ramornie
Mill

To Glenrothes
A914

Index to Newburgh

Abbey Road	D2
Abernethy Road	A2
Aipple Yaird	B2
Albany Terrace	C1
Anderson Street	B2
Back Manse (5)	C2
Bank Close	B2
Banklands	A3
Clatchard Court (2)	C2
Clinton Street	B2
Coach Road	C1
Cornhill Street	C2
Cupar Road	C2
East Shore Road	C1
Farmhouse, The	E1
Gardens Road	B2
Guthrie Court	C2
Guthrie Gardens	C2
High Street	B2
Hill Road	B2
Lindores Abbey Farm Cottages	E2
Lindores Court	B2
Livingstone Street	B2
Lyall Place	C2
Mason Street	B2
Melville Place	D2
Mid Shore Road	C2
Millhall Cottages	E3
Mitchell Street	C2
Moncrieff Way	C1
Monkswell Road	C3
Morris Place	D2
Mugdrum Place	B2
Neuk, The	C1
Parkhill	E1
Reef Mog (4)	C2
Robertson Crescent	C2
St Katherine's Court	B2
Scotland Terrace	C1
Shore, The	C1
Shorehead	C2
Shuttlefield Street	A2
Steading, The	E1
Sweerie	A2
Tay Street	C2
Tolbooth Close	C2
Towerwell (1)	B2
Towerwell Square	B2
West Port Road	B2
West Shore Road	B1
Whinpark Place (3)	C2
Whitecraig Road	C2
Woodriffe	A3
Woodriffe Road	A3
York Place	B1

Index to Pitlessie

Burnside	B1
Crossgates	B2
Cupar Road	B2
Dowlas Court	B1
High Street	B1
Ladybank Road	B1
Lister Place	C1
Malt Row	C1
Pitlessie Mill Road	B1
Priestfield Maltings	C1
Ramornie Mill Farm Cottages	A2
School View	B1
Wilkie Court	B1
Wynd, The	C1

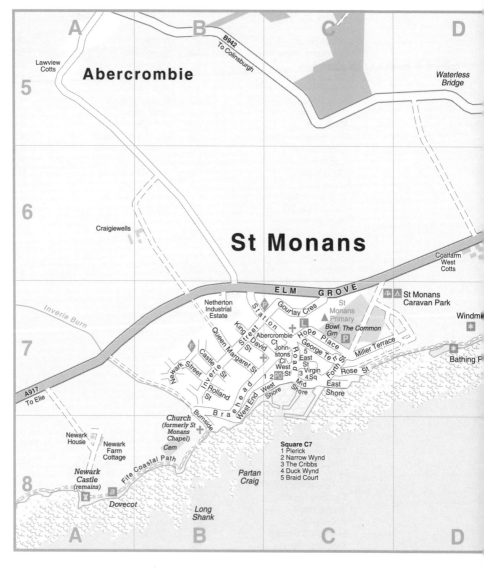

Index to Pittenweem

		Castle Street	B7	Elm Grove	C7	Kirkgate	C7
Abbey Wall Road	H5	Charles Street	G5	Forth Street	C7	Kirklatch Court	C7
Abercrombie Court	C7	Coalfarm West	D6	George Terrace	C7	Lady Wynd	C7
Backgate	G5	Cottages		Glebe Park	H5	Lawview Cottages	
Braehead	B7	Cove Wynd	G5	Gourlay Crescent	C7	Market Place	
Braehead Road	H5	Cribbs, The (3)	C7	Gyles, The	H6	Marygate	
Braid Court (5)	C7	David Street	G5	High Street	G6	Mayview	
Brown's Close	G5	Duck Wynd (4)	C7	Hope Place	C7	Mid Shore	
Bruce's Wynd	G6	East Shore		Inverie Street	G6	(Pittenweem)	B7
Burnside	B7	(Pittenweem)		James Street	G5	Mid Shore	
Calman's Wynd	G6	East Shore	C7	Johnstons Close	C7	(St Monans)	C7
Caiplie Craig	F5	(St Monans)		King David	B7	Miller Terrace	
		East Street	C7	Street		Milton Court	

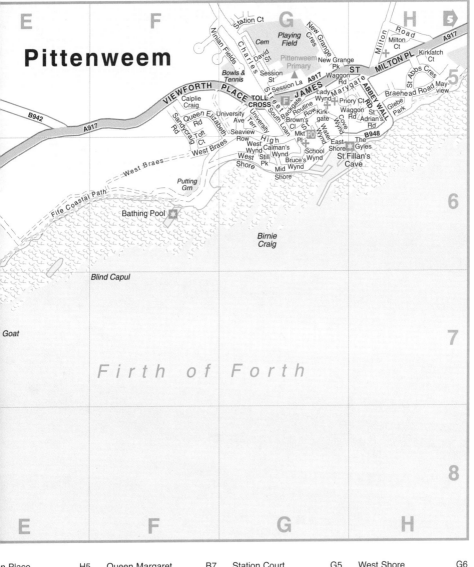

Pittenweem

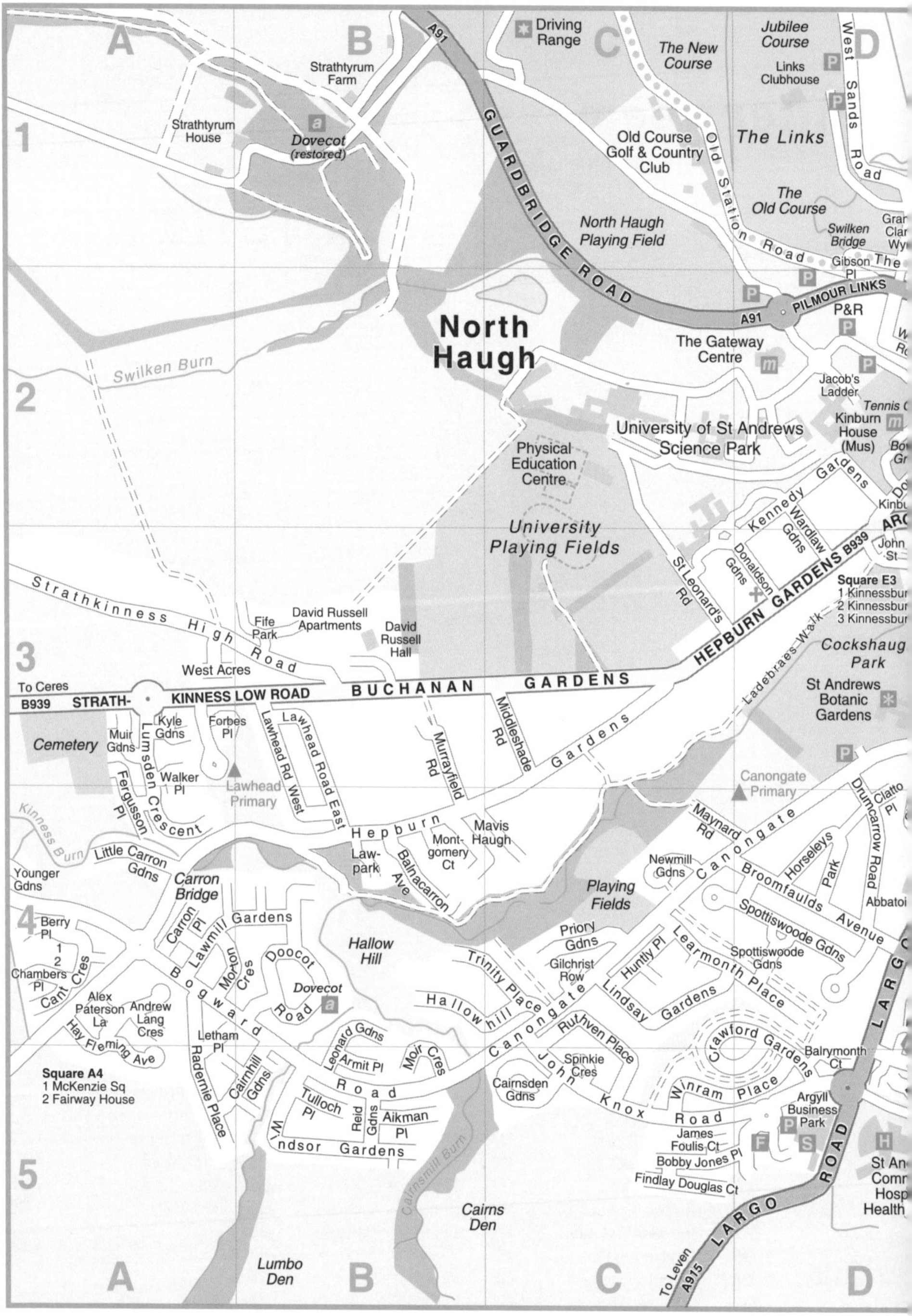

A
B
C
D
1
2
3
4
5
A91
Strathtyrum Farm
Strathtyrum House
Dovecot (restored)
Driving Range
The New Course
Jubilee Course
Links Clubhouse
West Sands Road
The Links
Old Course Golf & Country Club
Old Station Road
The Old Course
Swilken Bridge
Gibson Pl
GUARDBRIDGE ROAD
North Haugh Playing Field
PILMOUR LINKS
P&R
North Haugh
The Gateway Centre
Jacob's Ladder
Tennis
Kinburn House (Mus)
Swilken Burn
University of St Andrews Science Park
Physical Education Centre
Kennedy Gardens
Wardlaw Gdns
Donaldson Gdns
St Leonard's Rd
University Playing Fields
B939
HEPBURN GARDENS
John St
Square E3
1 Kinnessbur
2 Kinnessbur
3 Kinnessbur
Strathkinness High Road
Fife Park
David Russell Apartments
David Russell Hall
West Acres
Ladebraes Walk
Cockshaugh Park
St Andrews Botanic Gardens
To Ceres
B939
STRATH- KINNESS LOW ROAD
BUCHANAN GARDENS
Kyle Gdns
Forbes Pl
Muir Gdns
Lumsden Crescent
Lawhead Road East
Lawhead Rd West
Murrayfield Rd
Middleshade Rd
Gardens
Cemetery
Walker Pl
Lawhead Primary
Fergusson Pl
Canongate Primary
Kinness Burn
Hepburn
Mont-gomery Ct
Mavis Haugh
Maynard Rd
Drumcarrow Road
Clatto Pl
Little Carron Gdns
Law-park
Balnacarron Ave
Newmill Gdns
Canongate
Horseleys Park
Younger Gdns
Carron Bridge
Broomfaulds Avenue
Playing Fields
Abbatoi
Berry Pl
1
2
Chambers Pl
Cant Cres
Carron Pl
Lawmill Gardens
Morton Cres
Doocot Road
Hallow Hill
Priory Gdns
Spottiswoode Gdns
Trinity Place
Gilchrist Row
Huntly Pl
Learmonth Place
Spottiswoode Gdns
Alex Paterson La
Andrew Lang Cres
Bogward Road
Dovecot
Hallowhill
Lindsay Gardens
LARGO ROAD
Hay Fleming Ave
Letham Pl
Leonard Gdns
Armit Pl
Moir Cres
Ruthven Place
Spinkie Cres
Crawford Gardens
Balrymonth Ct
Square A4
1 McKenzie Sq
2 Fairway House
Radernie Place
Cairnhill Gdns
Tulloch Pl
Reid Gdns
Aikman Pl
Cairnsden Gdns
John Knox Road
Winram Place
Argyll Business Park
Windsor Gardens
James Foulis Ct
Bobby Jones Pl
Findlay Douglas Ct
Cairnsmill Burn
Cairns Den
Lumbo Den
To Leven
A915
LARGO

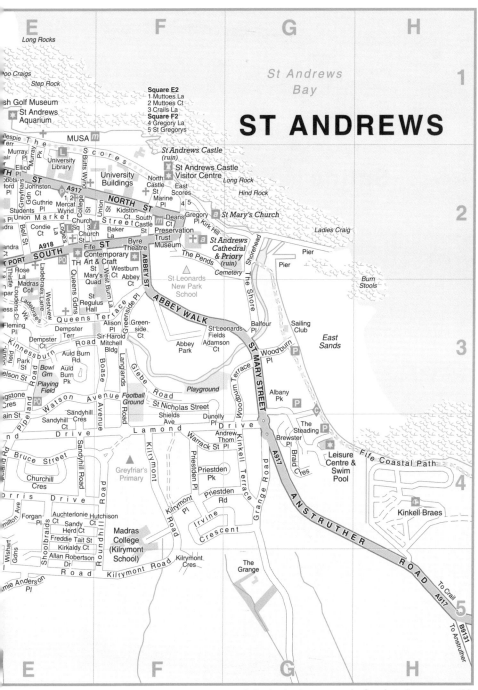

ST ANDREWS

St Andrews Bay

Square E2
1 Muttoes La
2 Muttoes Ct
3 Crails La
Square F2
4 Gregory La
5 St Gregorys

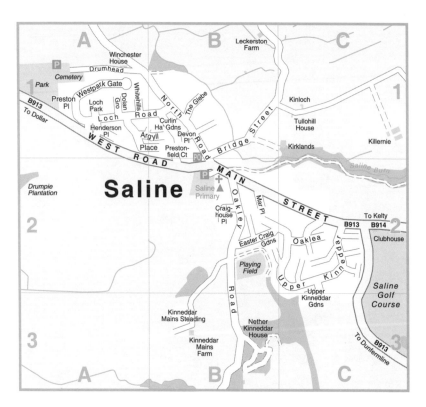

Saline

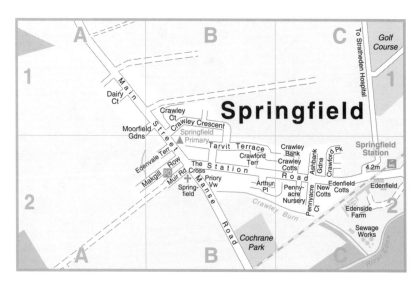

Springfield

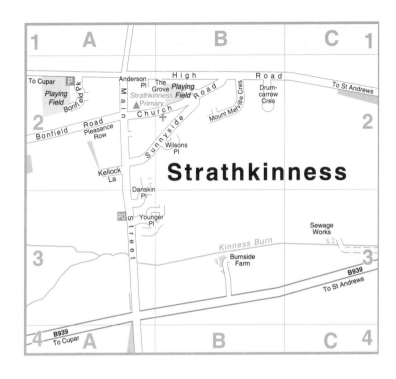

Index to Saline

Argyll Place	A1
Bridge Street	B1
Craighouse Place	B2
Curlin' Ha' Gardens	B1
Devon Place	B1
Dolan Grove	A1
Drumhead	A1
Easter Craig Gardens	B2
Glebe, The	B1
Henderson Place	A1
Kinneddar Mains Steading	B3
Loch Park	A1
Loch Road	A1
Main Street	B2
Mar Place	B2
North Road	B1
Oaklea	C2
Oakley Road	B2
Preston Place	A1
Prestonfield Court	B1
Upper Kinneddar Gardens	C2
Upper Kinneddar	C2

West Road	A1
Westpark Gate	A1
Whitehills	A1

Index to Springfield

Arthur Place	B2
Ashbank Gardens	C2
Crawford Park	C2
Crawford Terrace	B2
Crawley Bank	C2
Crawley Cottages	C2
Crawley Court	B1
Crawley Crescent	B1
Cross, The	B2
Dairy Court	A1
Edenfield Cottages	C2
Edenvale Terrace	B2
Main Street	A1
Makgill Row	B2
Manse Road	B2
Moorfield Gardens	A1
Muir Road	B2
New Cottages	C2

Pennyacre Court	C2
Pennyacre Nursery	C2
Priory View	B2
Springfield	B2
Station Road	B2
Tarvit Terrace	B2

Index to Strathkinness

Anderson Place	A2
Bonfield Park	A2
Bonfield Road	A2
Church Road	A2
Danskin Place	A3
Drumcarrow Crescent	B2
Grove, The	B2
High Road	B2
Kellock Lane	A2
Main Street	A2
Mount Melville Crescent	B2
Pleasance Row	A2
Sunnyside	A2
Wilsons Place	B2
Younger Place	A3

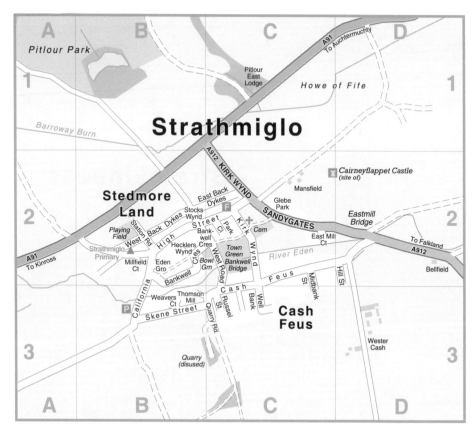

Index to Strathmiglo

Bankwell Crescent	B2	Stocks Wynd	B2	Craigmore Gardens	K2
California	B3	Thomson Mill	B3	Durham Terrace	H2
Cash Feus	C3	Weavers Court	B3	Eilean Lane	K2
East Back Dykes	C2	Well Bank	C3	Forthview Terrace	J2
East Mill Court	C2	West Back Dykes	B2	Gollet Way	L3
Eden Grove	B2	West Road	C2	Kay Road	L3
Hecklers Wynd	B2			Logan Road	L3
High Street	B2, D2	**Index to Torryburn**		Low Causeway	K2
Kirk Wynd	C2			Low Causewayside	H2
Midbank Street	C2	Adia Road	L3	Main Street	H2
Millfield Court	B2	Bayview	K2	Ness, The	K2
Park Close	C2	Beveridge Cottages	H2	Orchard Terrace	L2
Quarry Road	C3	Causeway Lane	K2	Rose Lane	K2
Russel Street	C3	Craigflower Court	K2	Rosemill Court	H2
Sandygates	C2	Craigflower Gardens	K2	Smiddy Wynd	H2
Skene Street	B3	Craigflower House	K3	Tinian Crescent	J2
Station Road	B2	Craigflower View	K3	Torry Bay Court	H2

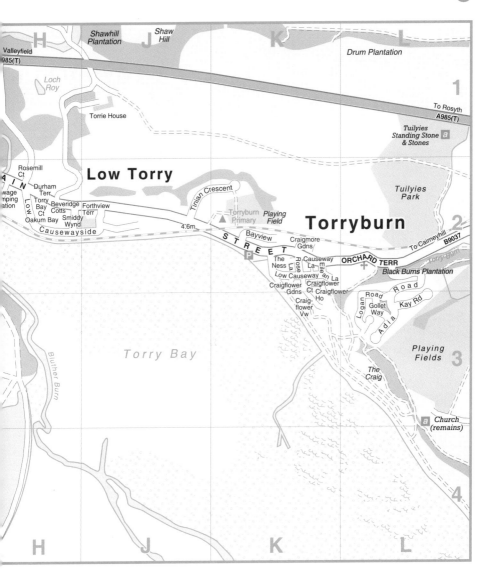

Shawhill Plantation

Shaw Hill

Drum Plantation

Valleyfield

985(T)

Loch Roy

To Rosyth

A985(T)

Torrie House

Tuilyies Standing Stone a & Stones

Rosemill Ct

Low Torry

AIN

wage mping ation

Durham Terr

Torry Bay Ct

Beveridge Cotts

Forthview Terr

Oakum Bay

Smiddy Wynd

Causewayside

Low

Tinian Crescent

4:6m

Torryburn Primary

Playing Field

Torryburn

Tuilyies Park

To Cairneyhill

B9037

STREET

Bayview

Craigmore Gdns

ORCHARD TERR

Torry burn

P

The Ness

Rose La

Causeway La

Ellean La

Black Burns Plantation

Low Causeway

Craigflower Gdns

Craigflower Ct

Craigflower Ho

Craig- flower Vw

Logan Road

Gollet Way

Road

Adia

Kay Rd

Torry Bay

Bluther Burn

The Craig

Playing Fields

a Church (remains)

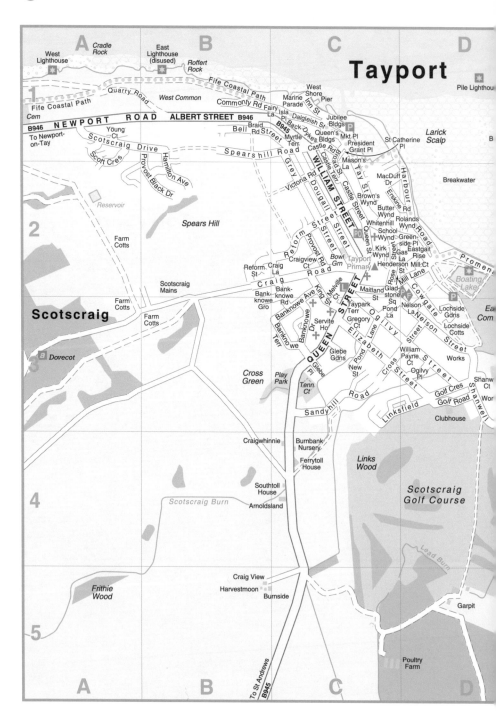

Tayport

Index to Tayport

Albert Street	B1	Market Place	C1
Back Dykes	C1	Marine Parade	C1
Banknowe Avenue	C3	Mason's Lane	C1
Banknowe Drive	C3	Melville Court	C2
Banknowe Grove	B3	Mill Court	D2
Banknowe Road	C2	Mill Lane	D2
Banknowe Terrace	C3	Myrtle Terrace	C1
Bell Street	B1	Nelson Lane	D3
Braid Road	B1	Nelson Street	D3
Broad Street	C1	New Street	C3
Brown's Wynd	C2	Newport Road	A1
Butter Wynd	C2	Ogilvy Place	D3
Castle Road	C1	Ogilvy Street	C3
Castle Street	C2	Pond Lane	C3
Castle Terrace	C1	President Grant Place	C1
Commonty Road	B1	Promenade	D2
Cowgate	D3	Provost Black Drive	B2
Craig Lane	C2	Provost Road	C2
Craig Road	C2	Quarry Road	A1
Craigview Court	C2	Queen Street	C3
Cross Street	C3	Queen's Buildings	C1
Dalgleish Street	C1	Reform Street	B2, C2
Dougall Street	C2	Rolands Wynd	D2
Eastgait Rise	D2	Rose Street	C2
Elizabeth Street	C3	St Catherine Place	C1
Erskine Road	C2	Sandyhill Road	C3
Fairy Lane	B1	School Wynd	C2
Farm Cottages	A2, A3, B3	Scotscraig Drive	A1
Gas Lane	D2	Scott Crescent	A1
Gladstone Square	C2	Servite House	C3
Glebe Gardens	C3	Shanwell Court	D3
Glebe Place	C3	Shanwell Road South	E4
Golf Crescent	D3	Shanwell Road	D3
Golf Road	D3	Spearshill Road	B1
Greenside Place	D2	Tay Street	C2
Gregory Court	C3	Taypark Terrace	C3
Grey Street	C2	Victoria Road	C2
Hamilton Avenue	B2	West Shore	C1
Harbour Road	D2	Whitenhill	C2
Henderson Street	C2	William Payne Court	D3
Inn Street	C1	William Street	C2
Isla Place	C1	Young Court	A1
Jubilee Buildings	C1		
King Street	C2		
Kirk Wynd	C2		
Links Court	D4		
Links Crescent	D4		
Links Road North	D3		
Links Road	D4		
Linksfield	C3		
Lochside Cottages	D3		
Lochside Gardens	D3		
Lundin Crescent	E4		
MacDuff Drive	C2		
Maitland Street	C2		

E

1

Tom's
Hole

White
Scalp

2

ad

3

BMX
Track

South
orks

Lundin
Bridge

Fife Coastal Path

4

5

E

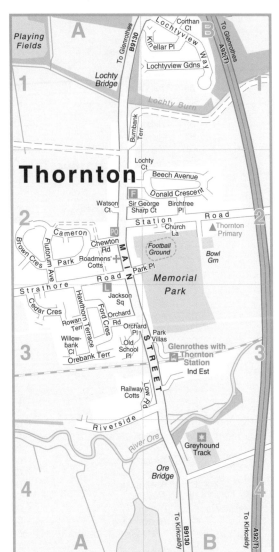

Index to Thornton

Beech Avenue	B2
Birchtree Place	B2
Brown Crescent	A2
Burnbank Terrace	A1
Cameron Park	A2
Cedar Crescent	A3
Chewton Road	A2
Church Lane	B2
Corthan Court	B1
Donald Crescent	B2
Flutorum Avenue	A2
Ford Crescent	A3
Hawthorn Terrace	A3
Jackson Square	A3
Kinellar Place	B1
Lochty Court	B2
Lochtyview Gardens	B1
Lochtyview Way	B1
Low Road	B3
Main Street	A2
Old School Place	A3
Orchard Place	A3
Orchard Road	A3
Orebank Terrace	A3
Park Place	A2
Park Villas	B3
Railway Cottages	A3
Riverside	A4
Roadmens' Cottages	A2
Rowan Terrace	A3
Sir George Sharp Court	A2
Station Road	B2
Strathore Road	A3
Watson Court	A2
Willowbank Close	A3

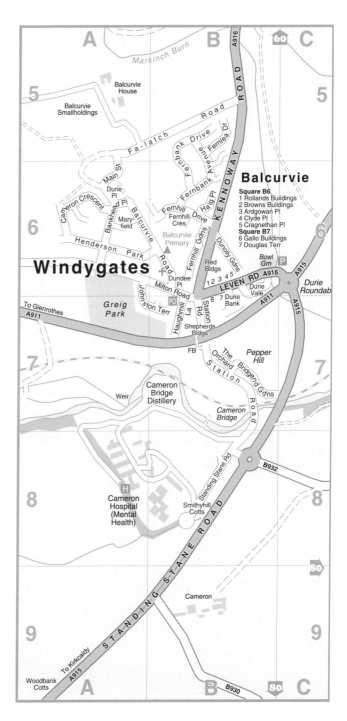

Index to Windygates

rdgowan Place (3)	B6
alcurvie Road	A6
ankhead Place	A6
ridgend Gardens	B7
rowns Buildings (2)	B6
ameron Crescent	A6
lyde Place (4)	B6
ragnethan Place (5)	B6
ouglas Terrace (7)	B7
undee Place	B6
unolly Gardens	B6
urie Bank	B7
urie Place	A6
urie Vale	B6
a-latch Road	A5
ernbank Avenue	B6
ernbank Drive	B6
ernhill Crescent	B6
ernhill Drive	B6
ernhill Gardens	B6
ernlea Drive	B5
allo Buildings (6)	B7
aig Place	B6
aughmill Lane	B7
enderson Park	A6
ohnston Terrace	A6
ennoway Road	B6
even Road	B7
ain Street	A6
aryfield	A6
ilton Road	B6
rchard, The	B7
ed Buildings	B6
ollands Buildings (1)	B6
hepherds Buildings	B7
mithyhill Cottages	B8
anding Stane Road	A9, B8
ation Road	B6
oodbank Cottages	A9

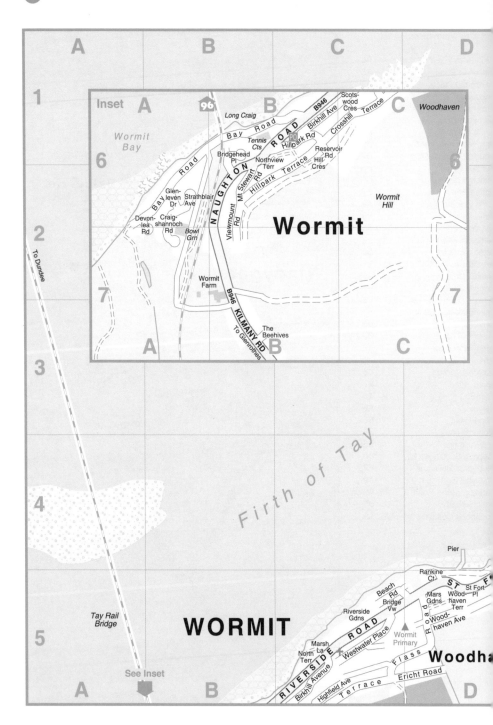

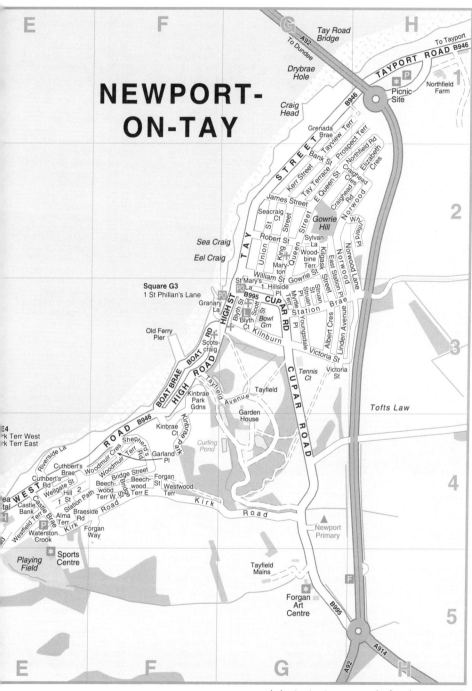

Index to street names can be found on page 110

Index to Cowdenbeath

Acorn Road 24 C5
Alexander Street 25 E6
Allan Park 25 B10
Anderson Drive 24 C9
Arthur Court 25 E8
Arthur Place 25 E8
Arthur Street 25 E8
Ash Grove 24 C7
Barclay Street 24 C8
Beath View Road 24 B9
Birchbank 24 C9
Blackburn Drive 24 B8
Blamey Crescent 24 C8
Bowling Green Street 24 D7
Braemount 24 B9
Bridge End Cottages 25 F5
Bridge Street 25 E8
Broad Street 24 C9
Broomfield Road 24 D6
Brucefield Terrace 25 G5
Burgh Road 25 E7
Burnside Terrace 24 B9
Cedar Crescent 25 E5
Centenary Place 24 C5
Chambers Court 25 E7
Chapel Street 24 D8
Cherry Place 24 D8
Church Street 25 E8
Copeland Crescent 24 C8
Cowden Place 25 B11
Craigbeath Court 24 C6
Craigton Place 24 D9
Cuddyhouse Road 24 A8
Cullaloe View 24 D9
Dalbeath Crescent 24 B9
Dalbeath Gardens 25 A10
Dora Court 25 E5
Downfield 24 D5
Drylie Court 24 C7
Drylie Street 24 C7
Elgin Road 25 E7
Erskine Street 25 H5
Ewing Street 24 C9
Factory Road 25 E7
Farm Road 24 C8
Foote Street 25 H5
Foulford Place 24 C7
Foulford Road 24 C7
Foulford Street 24 D7
Fountain Place 25 E8
Furnace Place 25 F5
Gagarin Way 25 F5
Gallacher Place 25 F5
Gardiner Place 24 C9
Gardiner Road 24 D9
Gateside Court 24 B8
George Street 24 C7
Gilmour Street 25 E5
Glenfarg Crescent 25 E6
Glenfield Avenue 24 D5
Glenfield Court 24 D6
Glenfield Crescent 24 D6
Glenfield Gardens 24 D6

Glenfield Road 24 D6
Golf Course Road 24 D5
Gordon Street 25 E5
Gray Park 24 D5
Greenbank Drive 24 B9
Greenmount 24 B9
Hall Street 24 D7
Hanover Court 24 D7
Hawthorn Crescent 25 A10
High Street 25 E7
Hill Street 24 D7
Hillcrest 24 C8
Hillview 24 C8
  (Cowdenbeath)
Hillview 25 B10
  (Hill of Beath)
Hilton Lane 24 C5
Hilton View 25 F5
Hope Street 25 F5
James Court 24 D9
James Street 24 D9
Johnston Park 24 C6
Keir Street 24 B7
King Street 24 C7
Kirkford Court 24 B7
Kirkton Place 24 C6
Leuchatsbeath Drive 24 C6
Lochgelly Road 25 E5
Main Street 25 B10
  (Hill of Beath)
Main Street 25 E5
  (Lumphinnans)
Marshall Street 25 E8
Maxwell Crescent 24 B9
Meadowfield 24 D5
Meldrum Court 24 D8
Milne Crescent 24 C8
Mitchell Crescent 25 B10
Mossbank 24 C9
Mossend Terrace 24 C9
Moss-side Road 24 C8
Natal Place 24 D8
Netherbeath Road 25 A11
Netherton Road 24 C5
No. 7 Pit Road 24 D7
Northfield 24 D5
Ochil View 25 F5
Old Perth Road 24 A5, B9
Park Avenue 24 D8
Park Place 25 A11
Park Road 24 C8
Park Street 24 D8
Park View 25 B10
Patterson Lane 25 E8
Paul Place 25 E7
Paul Street 25 H5
Perth Road 24 D5
Pilkham Court 24 D8
Pit Road 25 F5
Polworth Place 25 E7
Pretoria Place 24 C7
Primmer Place 25 E8
Primrose Lane 24 D6
Prospect Street 24 C7
Quarry Court 24 C8

Rae Street 24 C9
Raith Avenue 24 D8
Randolph Street 25 E8
Robert Smith Court 25 F5
Rose Street 24 D9
Rosebank 25 E7
Rosehill Crescent 24 C8
Rowan Terrace 24 D8
Russell Street 24 C7
School Street 25 E8
Seco Place 25 E7
Selkirk Avenue 24 D9
Shamrock Place 24 C7
Sinclair Drive 24 C8, C9
Small Street 25 H5
Smith Avenue 24 C8
South Street 24 D9
Southfield 24 D6
Station Road 25 E7
Stein's Place 24 D8
Stenhouse Street 24 C7
Stuart Place 25 E6
Sunnyside Court 25 E7
Sunnyside Place 25 H5
Swintons Place 25 A10
Sycamore Crescent 25 E5
Taylor Avenue 24 C7
Terris Place 25 E8
Thistle Street 25 E8
Torbeith Gardens 25 A10
Tulloch Court 24 C6
Union Street 25 E7
Valleyfield Place 25 E6
Viewfield Terrace 25 F5
Walker Street 24 C8
  (Cowdenbeath)
Walker Street 25 H5
  (Lochgelly)
Wallace Street 24 D8
Wardlaw Street 24 D8
Watson Street 25 E8
Weir Avenue 24 C9
Wemyss Street 25 E8
West Lane 24 C9
Westburn Avenue 24 C9
William Sharp Place 25 E6
Wilson Street 24 D7
Woodbank 24 C9
Woodend Place 25 B10
Woodend Place 24 C9
Woodside 24 D8
Wyre Hayes 25 B10
  Cottages
Young Court 24 D8
Young Terrace 24 C8

Index to Cupar

Adamson Court 30 D2
Angus Place 30 C2
Ashlar Lane 30 D3
Ashlar Park 30 D3
Back Lebanon 30 D2
Balgarvie Court 30 C2

Balgarvie Crescent 3
Balgarvie Road 3
Balmerino Place (6) 3
Bank Street 3
Bathgate Court 3
Beech Bank
Beechgrove Rise
Belfield Gardens 3
Bell Close (8)
Betts Close (3)
Bishopgate
Blalowan Gardens
Blalowan Park
Bobber Wynd
Bonar Court
Bonnygate
Bonvil Row
Bowling Green Road
Braehead
Brighton Place
Brighton Road
Burn Close
Burnside Close (4)
Burnside North
Campbell Crescent
Carslogie Road
Castle Street
Castlebank Gardens
Castlebank Road
Castlefield
Castlehill Place
Castlehill
Ceres Road
Charles Jarvis Court
Cherry Lane
Clair Wood Place
Clash Close (16)
Coal Road
Commerce Street
Constable Acre
County Houses
Cow Brae
Crichton Way
Cross Keys Close (7)
Crossgate
Cupar Mills
Cupar Road
Curling Pond Court
Dalgairn Crescent
Dalgleish Gardens
Davidson Place
Drum Road
Drum Well
Drumdryan Place
Drummond Court
Drysdale Gardens
East Bridge
East Burnside
East Moat Hill
East Road 31
Eden Court
Eden Park
Edenbank Road
Ferguson Square (12)
Ferniehall Cottages

ield	30 C4	Provost Scott Court	30 D3	Alburne Crescent	48 L6
rs, The	31 E2	Provost Wynd	30 D3	Alburne Park	48 L6
Lebanon	30 D2	Quarry Road	30 A5	Alder Lane	47 G6
bank Crescent	31 E5	Railway Place	31 E3	Alexander Rise	51 H7
e Govan Road	30 B3	Rattray Place	30 C2	Alexander Road	51 H7
e Inn Pend	30 D2	Rigg's Place	31 E3	Alexandra Crescent	49 N6
ardens	31 F2	Riverside Court	31 E2	Alford Drive	51 E7
n Park	31 E1	Robertson Road	31 F4	Aline Court	51 F8
ton Place	30 D3	Rollo's Close (15)	30 D3	Allan Street	46 C5
d Court	30 D2	Rose Terrace	30 D1	Almond Path	47 G6
urton Place	30 C4	St Catherine Street	31 E2	Almond Way	47 G6
n Mill	30 D4	St Mary's Road	30 B2	Altyre Avenue	52 K9
ount Park	30 C2	St Michaels Drive	31 E3	Altyre Court	52 K9
Close	30 D1	Sandylands Road	31 E5	Alves Drive	50 D8
escent	30 D2	Scotstarvit View	30 C4	Alwyn Green	47 G3
reet	30 C2	Short Lane	30 D3	Alyth Court	48 K3
th Drive	31 F4	Skinners Steps	30 D2	Ancrum Court	47 E5
Park	31 E3	South Bridge	31 E3	Anderson Drive	46 B5
on Court	30 D2	South Road	30 D5	Anderson Place	51 G8
s Ingles	30 B3	South Road	31 E3	Annandale Gardens	50 D6
cent		South Union Street	30 D3	Ardgartan Court	48 K3
s Place	31 E4	Speedie's Close (11)	31 E3	Ardoch Park	47 F3
Place	30 C3	Spruce Gardens	30 A5	Ardross Court	51 H8
on Crescent	30 C1	Station Road	31 E3	Ardross Place	51 H8
om Court	30 D2	Steele's Close (10)	31 E2	Argyll Place	47 G3
s Crescent	30 C2	Sun Close (9)	31 E2	Ashbank Court	52 J11
s Drive	30 C1	Tannage Close (13)	31 E3	Ashley Road	51 G10
s Park	30 C2	Tarvit Avenue	31 F3	Ashtree Path (4)	52 L7
ynd	30 D3	Tarvit Cottages	31 G3	Aspen Avenue	47 G4
te	30 D3	Tarvit Court	31 F3	Atholl Way	47 F4
nds Park	30 C1	Tarvit Drive	31 F2	Auchanan Gardens	52 H11
Gardens	31 E4	Tarvit Gardens	31 F3	Auchmithie Place	52 H11
Vynd	30 D2	Temperance	30 D2	Auchmuty Drive	48 J6
urn Place	30 D2	Close (5)		Auchmuty Road	52 J7
e Gardens	31 F2	Thomaston Drive	31 F2	Ayton Court	47 E5
on Terrace	30 D2	Trynlaw Gardens	30 A5	Back Row	46 C5
e Drive	30 C4	Upper Dalgairn	30 D2	Croftouterly	
Lane	30 D3	Waterend Road	31 E3	Baigillie Court	48 J4
en Park	31 E4	Watt's Gardens	31 F1	Bailies Wynd (2)	49 N5
en's Close (14)	31 E3	Well Place	31 E2	Baird Road	52 L8
li Place	31 F3	Well Street	31 E2	Balbirnie Avenue	49 M5
ay Court (1)	30 C2	Wemyss Place	31 E4	Balbirnie Court	49 N5
es Gardens	31 E1	West Park Road	30 C3	Balbirnie Rise	52 K7
nd Drive	30 D3	West Port	30 C3	Balbirnie Road	52 K8
field Place	31 E4	Westfield Avenue	30 C3	Balbirnie Street	49 N5
wside Road	31 E3	Westfield Road	30 B3, C3	Baldinnie Place	51 H11
nvil	30 C2	Westport Place	30 C3	Balfarg Farm	48 L2
field Brae	31 E1	Wide Pend (17)	30 D3	Cottages	
k Park	30 D4	Winthank Court	30 D3	Balfour Gardens	51 G9
k	30 C3			Balgeddie Close	47 F3
d	30 C4			Balgeddie Court	47 E3
e	30 D4	**Index to Glenrothes, Leslie**		Balgeddie Farm	47 E3
ll Road	30 C2	**& Markinch**		Cottages	
ve Avenue	30 C3			Balgeddie Gardens	47 E3
ie Bank	30 D4	Abbotsford Drive	51 E7	Balgeddie Grove	47 F3
Cabra (2)	30 D2	Aboyne Way	47 F3	Balgeddie Park	47 E3
lose	30 D3	Achray Park	48 K3	Balgeddie Way	47 E3
wn	30 D2	Acorn Court	53 J7	Balgonie Avenue	52 L7
son Cottages	30 C2	Adamson Place	51 G7	Balgonie Place	49 N5
son Court	31 E2	Adrian Road	51 G7	(Markinch)	
Jnion Street	30 D2	Affric Road	48 K3	Balgonie Place	52 L7
ale	31 F2	Ailort Place	51 F7	(Woodside)	
dgate	30 D3	Aitken Road	48 H4	Balgonie Road	49 N6
ent Square	30 D3	Albany Gate	53 J6	Ballater Green	47 F3
ie Road	31 F2	Alburne Court	48 L6	Ballinbreich Terrace	46 D4

Ballingall Drive	47 E4
Ballingall Park	47 F4
Balmanno Green	52 J11
Balmoral Road	52 J11
Balnagowan Drive	51 H8
Balsillie Avenue	46 A2, C4
Baltimore Road	51 F9
Banchory Green	47 F2
Bank Place	46 B5
Bankhead Avenue	53 M10
Barnhill Place	50 D7
Barnton Place	50 C7
Barony Place	46 D5
Barrie Path	51 G6
Baxter Road	53 J7
Bayes Path	51 G8
Beaufort Drive	51 H9
Beaufort Drive	52 J8, K9
Beauly Court	51 F7
Beckman Street	51 G7
Beeches, The	52 K7
Beechwood Avenue	47 H5
Beechwood Court	47 H5
Beechwood Drive	47 H5
Beechwood Park	47 H5
Beechwood Place	47 H5
Benalder Court	48 K3
Bennachie Court	48 K3
Benvane Road	47 E2
Berryhill	51 H10
Bethune Path	51 H7
Bethune Road	52 H7
Betson Street	49 N5
Bevan Court	51 G7
Bighty Avenue	52 L7
Bighty Court	52 L7
Bighty Crescent	52 L7
Bighty Road	52 L7
Bilsland Path North	51 G7
Bilsland Path South	51 G7
Bilsland Road	51 F7
Birchtree Road	52 K8
Blackadder Court	47 H2
Blackwood Drive	53 M10
Blackwood	53 M9, M11
Road	
Blackwood Way	53 M10
Blair Avenue	52 J10
Blair Court	52 J10
Blair Place	46 C5
Blairadam Court	48 K3
Blanche Path	47 H4
Boblingen Way	51 E9
Boblingen Way	52 J8, K7
Bonnyton Court	52 H11
Boston Road	51 G9
Bow Butts	49 N4
Bowery, The	46 D5
Bowling Green	49 N5
Road	
Bradgate Gardens	47 E4
Brae Court	47 G3
Braehead Way	47 F4
Braemar Court	51 G9
Braemar Gardens	51 G8, G9

Name	Ref	Name	Ref	Name	Ref	Name	Ref
Brahan Park	52 J8	Chewton Way	51 E8	Dovecot Road	52 J7	Formonthills Road	
Braid Drive	52 J8	Chisholm Place	51 G6	Drum Close	52 J11	Forres Drive	
Breadalbane Crescent	47 F4	Church Street	53 H7	Drumlie Gardens	52 H11	Forrester's Gait	
Brent Place	47 G3	Claymore Court	47 H3	Drummond Place	51 F7	Forth Court	
Brodie Court	52 J11	Claymore Drive	47 G3	Duart Place	52 L9	Foxton Drive	5
Broom Road	51 F8	Claymore Path	47 G3	Duich Place	51 F7	Frances Path	
Bruce Road	52 J7	Cluny Place	52 J9	Dunbar Court	46 D6	Fraser Place	
Brunton Court	49 N5	Clyde Court	51 F7	Dunbeath Drive	52 J9	Front Row	
Brunton Drive	49 N5	Coaltown Road	49 N6	Duncan Road	51 H7	Croftouterly	
Brunton Gardens	49 N5	Colinton Court	47 F4	Dundas Place	51 F7	Fullerton Path	
Brunton Park	49 N5	Colliston Avenue	52 J9	Dunecht Court	47 F2	Fullerton Road	
Brunton Place	49 N5	Collydean Way	47 G3	Dunedin Place	49 M5	Fyne Court	
Brunton Quadrant	52 J7	Colonsay Park	47 H3	Dunlin Avenue	47 G3	Fyvie Green	5
Brunton Road	49 N5	Colquhoun Avenue	47 H2	Dunrobin Road	52 K10	Gare Place	
Buchan Path	47 G6	Commercial Street	49 N5	Dunstaffnage Place	52 J9	Garry Court	
Buchanan Road	51 H7	Conland Court	47 E2	Dunvegan Court	51 F8	Garvald Way	
Bucksburn Park	47 F2	Cornel Lane	47 H4	Dura Crescent	52 L7	George Street	
Burleigh Court	52 K10	Cornhill Road	52 J10	Dura Park	52 L7	Gibbs Close (1)	
Burnbank Terrace	L12	Coronation Street	53 P8	Durness Court	51 F8	Gifford Court	
Burns Road	53 G6	Cortachy Place	51 H11	Durris Drive	51 E7	Gilmour Court	
Burrelton Court	52 L11	Corthan Court	53 M11	Durward Drive	50 D8	Glamis Avenue	
Bute Gate	53 H6	Cos Lane	52 K8	Dyce Way	47 F3	Glamis Court	5
Bute Place	47 H3	Courthill Drive	51 H11	Eardley Court	47 H2	Glass Street	
Cabbagehall Place	46 C6	Cowal Crescent	47 F4	Earlston Way	46 D6	Glebe Place	
Cable Road	51 G9	Craigellachie Court	48 K3	Easton Place	51 F6	Glenartney Court	
Cadham Court	48 J4	Craigievar Drive	52 J9	Eden Crescent	53 M7	Glendarvel Place	
Cadham Crescent	48 J4	Craik Terrace	49 N4	Edensmuir Court	48 J3	Glendevon Road	5
Cadham Road	47 G4	Cramond Way	47 F4	Edison House	53 H6	Gleneagles Avenue	
Cadham Square	48 J4	Crannag Court	48 H4	Ednam Drive	47 E6	Glengarry Court	
Cadham Terrace	48 J4	Crathes Close	52 J11	Elgin Drive	50 D7	Glenmore Court	
Cadham Villas	48 J4	Crawford Place	51 F6	Elliot Place	47 F6	Glenorchy Court	
Cadzow Place	47 F7	Crinan Place	51 G7	Ellon Park	47 F3	Glentress Gardens	
Cairngorm Drive	47 F2	Croft Crescent	49 N4	Elm Lane	47 G5	Glenurquhart Court	
Calder Court	47 H1	Croft Road (Leslie)	46 C5	Elm View	49 N5	Glenwood Road	
Caledonia House	51 G8	Croft Road (Markinch)	49 N5	Elrick Park	47 F2	Glover Road	
Cameron Crescent	47 F6	Croft Villas	49 N4	Eriskay Square	47 H3	Golf Course Road	
Campbell Place	51 F6	Cromarty Court	51 E7	Errol Gardens	47 G3	Golf Course Road	
Canmore Path	52 J7	Cromdale Brae	47 F2	Erskine Place	51 H7	Granton Court	
Canmore Place	53 J7	Crompton Road	51 E10	Etive Place	51 G7	Green, The	
Canmore Road	53 H7	Crowlin Avenue	47 H3	Ettrick Way	46 D6	Greenlaw Crescent	
Canmore Walk	53 H7	Culbin Court	48 K2	Evandale Court	51 E8	Greenmantle Place	
Cardean Way	47 F3	Culdees Avenue	47 F3	Falcon Drive	52 K7	Greenmantle Way	
Carfrae Drive	47 E6	Cullen Drive	50 D7	Falcon Gardens	52 K7	Greenside	
Carleton Avenue	53 M7	Culzean Place	52 J10	Falcon Path	52 K7	Greenside Court	
Carleton Crescent	53 M7	Cumbrae Park	47 H3	Falkland Court	53 H6	Greenside Place	
Carlyle Road	51 G7	Cunningham Place	51 F7	Falkland Gate	53 H6	Greenwell Park	
Carnbee Place	51 H11	Dalton Road	51 G10	Falkland Place	53 H6	Greystone Park	
Carnegie Place	51 G7	Darnaway Drive	48 K3	Falkland Square	53 H6	Grieve Court	
Carnoustie Gardens	50 B8	David Road	51 H7	Faraday Road	51 E10	Groves Place	
Carrick Gate	53 H7	Davidson Place	51 F7	Ferguson Place	51 F7	Guthrie Court	
Carron Place	51 F7	Delgatie Avenue	52 K9	Fernie Court	52 K11	Guthrie Crescent	
Carseggie Crescent	52 L7	Delgatie Court	52 L9	Ferryden Place	51 H11	Haddington Crescent	
		Demarco Drive	47 H2	Fettykil Path	46 D5	Hamilton Place	
Caskieberran Drive	51 E9, G8	Denholm Court	46 D6	Findon Lane	48 K3	Hanover Court	
		Detroit Road	51 F9	Fingask Avenue	52 K10	Happer Crescent	
Caskieberran Road	51 E7, F8	Docherty Gardens	47 G5	Fleming Place	47 G4	Harris Way	
		Dornoch Place	51 E7	Flemington Road	48 J6	Hatton Green	
Cavendish Way	50 D11	Dorran Square	46 C4	Floors Court	52 J11	Hawthorn Path (2)	
Cawdor Drive	51 E7	Doubledikes Road	53 P9, P10	Floors Road	52 J11	Hazel Hill	
Cedar Drive	47 G4	Douglas Place	51 F7	Fordell Road	48 H4	Hazel Place	
Central Avenue	53 J6	Douglas Road	46 C5	Formonthills Court	47 E2	Heather Court	
Charleston Drive	52 L11	Dovecot Lane	52 J7	Formonthills Lane	47 E2	Heather Path	
Cherry Avenue	47 F6	Dovecot Park	52 K7	Formonthills Park	47 E2	Hedley House	
				Formonthills Road	46 D2	Heimdal Gardens	

erson Place	49 N5	Kingsmuir Gardens	52 L11	Lundin Crescent	51 H8	Mount Pleasant	46 B6
e, The	48 K2	Kinkell Avenue	51 H8	Lundin Place	51 H7	Muirdrum Gardens	52 L11
Court	50 D6	Kinloch Drive	52 K11	Lyle Avenue	52 J7	Muirfield Drive	50 C7
tage Green	52 K11	Kinnaird Close	51 H11	Lyle Crescent	52 J7	Munduff Drive	49 N5
Street (Leslie)	46 C5	Kinnordy Place	52 J11	Lyon Square	53 H6	Munro Court	47 G5
Street	49 N5	Kintail Court	47 F4	Lyon Way	53 H6	Munro Place	47 G6
kinch)		Kintore Park	47 F3	MacDuff Gardens	52 J7	Murchison Court	47 G3
ace	49 M4	Kintyre Gate	53 J7	MacDuff Road	52 J7	Murchison Path	47 G3
rrace	49 N4	Kirk Brae	49 N5	Mackie Crescent	49 M6	Murdoch Place	47 F6
ew	52 K8	Kirk Drive	46 B5	Mackie Gardens	49 M6	Murray Place	46 C5
nrothes)		Kirk Street	49 N4	MacTaggart Way	47 H3	Myres Drive	52 K10
ew	50 A11	Kirk Wynd	49 N4	McInnes Road	49 M6	Myrtle Avenue	47 G6
glassie)		Kirkinch Road	52 J11	Magnus Drive	47 G2	Nairn Path	51 G7
ree Road	52 L8	Kishorn Court	47 G1	Main Street	53 N9	Napier Place	53 G6
Square	47 H3	Lady Alice Path	48 H4	Malcolm Road	52 H7	Napier Road	51 E7
ood Avenue	47 E4	Lady Nina Cottages	53 N9	Mamore Road	48 K3	Napier Road	47 G6
on Avenue	47 H2	Lady Nina Square	53 P8	Mannering Court	50 D8	Nasmyth Road	50 D10
gate Gardens	49 N5	Lady's Walk	53 M8	Manse Road	49 N4	Netherby Park	47 F3
gtower Park	47 E4	Laggan Crescent	47 H2	Mansfield	46 B5	Nevis Place	51 F7
y Drive	50 D7	Lammermoor Court	51 F8	Maple Place	47 F6	Newark Place	53 M9
mans Court	48 J4	Landel Street	49 N6	Mar Drive	52 J11	Newark Road North	52 L9
man's Road	48 H4, J2	Langholm Crescent	47 E6	Marchmont Crescent	47 E5	Newark Road South	52 L9
r	49 Q2	Larch Avenue	47 G4	Marchmont Gate	53 H7	Newton Farm	49 N3
airnie	50 B11	Lauder Court	47 E6	Maree Way	47 H2	Cottages	
galows		Laurel Bank Drive	49 N5	Marmion Drive	51 E8	Newton Road	48 L3
eith Court	48 J4	Laurel Gardens	52 L8	Maryfield Crescent	46 C5	Ninian Quadrant	53 H7
Avenue	46 A5	Laurieston Park	48 K2	Maryfield Gardens	46 C5	Norman Place	46 C5
Road	51 F7	Laurence Park	50 A11	Matheson Place	51 F6	North Street	53 H6
Place	51 G7	Laverock Avenue	52 K7	Maxwell Place	47 F6	(Town Centre)	
ray Avenue	52 J9	Laverock Path	52 K7	Meadow Path	46 C5	North Street	46 C5
eillor Gardens	52 L11	Laverock Terrace	52 K7	Meadow View	49 Q2	(Markinch)	
ark	48 H4	Laxford Road	51 G7	Mearns Court	48 K3	Northall Road	49 N4
e Drive	51 E8	Lennox Court	47 G3	Megginch Place	52 K9	Northmuir Place	52 K11
s Watt Avenue	52 L10	Leslie Mains	47 F5	Meldrum Court	47 F2	Ochiltree Court	51 E8
Place	50 D8	Leslie Road	47 G5, H6	Melford Place	51 F7	Oldany Road	48 H4
ne Court	52 K8	Leven Place	53 M7	Melrose Court	47 E5	Old Balfarg Road	48 K2
rgh Court	51 E6	Leven Valley	49 M5	Melvich Place	51 F8	Orchard Drive	48 L6
Gray Path	48 J4	Gardens		Melville Close	52 K10	Orchard, The	46 D5
e Lee Lane	47 G5	Liberton Place	47 F4	Methlick Brae	47 F3	Osprey Road	50 B10
Dixon Court	49 N5	Lilac Path (3)	52 L7	Methven Drive	48 K3	Over Stenton	51 G10
Knox Gardens	48 H2	Limekilns, The	47 E3	Mey Green	52 J11	Cottages	
Ross Place	53 P9	Lindsay Place	51 H8	Michael Path	48 J4	Park Circle	49 M5
tone Path	47 G5	Linton Court	46 D6	Mid Row Croftouterly	46 C5	Park Lane	47 H2
e Grove	47 G6	Lismore Court	47 H4	Millburn Avenue	53 P9	Park Terrace	49 M5
e House	51 G8	Lochaber Court	47 F4	Milnwood Court	51 E8	Park View	49 M5
Court	48 J4	Locheil Court	48 J3	Minto Crescent	47 E6	Paterson Park	46 B5
Road	48 J4	Locheil Gardens	48 J3	Minto Place	51 E7	Pennan Place	47 F3
er Hill	47 G4	Lochnagar Court	47 F2	Mitchel Place	49 N5	Pentland Court	51 G8
Melons Avenue	48 L3	Lochty Court	50 A11	Mitchel Terrace	49 N5	Pentland House	51 G8
Drive	50 D7	Lochty Park	50 A11	Moffat Court	47 E5	Pentland Park	51 G8
Court	52 K11	Loch Katrine	51 F8	Moidart Drive	47 G2	Pentland Road	51 F8
Court	46 D6	Gardens		Moir Place	47 F6	Peploe Drive	47 H2
ay Drive	47 F3	Loch Venacher	51 F8	Monk's Walk Path	46 D4	Pine Lane	47 G5
orth Drive	51 E8	Gardens		Monk's Walk	46 D5	Pinkerton Road	51 H8
dy Road	51 H7	Lodge Rise	47 G4	Montrose Green	47 G2	Piper Drive	47 G3
a Place	48 H4	Lomond View	46 B5	Morar Court	51 F8	Pitcairn Avenue	47 F2, H2
hael Road	48 K3	(Leslie)		Moray Place	51 F7	Pitcairn Park	47 F2
ven Gardens	52 J11	Lomond View	52 L7	Morlich Gardens	47 G2	Pitcoudie Avenue	48 H4
r Place	M12	(Woodside)		Morrison Place	47 F6	Pitkevy Court	47 E2
dward	49 M6	Lorne Court	51 F7	Morsehead Place	46 D5	Pitkevy Gardens	46 D2
t		Lothian Court	47 E5	Morven Park	47 G4	Pitmedden Loan	47 F3
om Avenue	53 H6	Lovat Road	52 L10	Mount Frost Drive	48 L5	Pitteuchar Drive	51 H8
ssie Road	50 B10	Loyne Court	47 G2	Mount Frost Gardens	48 L5	Poplar Road	52 K8
ssie Road	51 G10	Lumsden Road	53 G7	Mount Frost Place	48 L5	Postgate	53 H7

Prestonhall Avenue	48 L5	Sappi Road	48 L6
Prestonhall Drive	48 L5	Scaraben Crescent	47 F2
Prestonhall Road	48 L5	School Road	53 P9
Prinlaws Road	46 B6	School Street	49 N4
Prinlaws Road	50 A6	Scotstarvit Place	51 H10
Provost's Land	46 C5	Scott Path North	51 G7
Pyetree Road	53 P9	Scott Path South	51 G7
Queen Margaret	52 H7	Scott Road	51 F6
Drive		Seath Court	46 C5
Queens Crescent	49 N6	Secret Garden, The	47 F3
Queen's Meadow	53 N9	Selkirk Place	49 N4
Queensgate	48 H6	(Markinch)	
Queensway	48 K6	Selkirk Place	51 H7
Raeburn Heights	51 G7	(Glenrothes)	
Raeburn Path	53 G7	Selkirk Street	49 N6
Ralston Court	50 C7	Seton Path	52 J7
Ramsay Court	46 B5	Seton Road	52 J7
Ramsay Gardens	46 B5	Shiel Court	51 F8
Ramsden Road	51 E11	Shin Court	48 K3
Randolph Path	48 J4	Shuna Square	48 H4
Rannoch Road	48 K3	Sinclair Avenue	51 F7
Rashleigh Court	51 E8	Skene Court	47 F3
Ratagan Court	48 K3	Skibo Avenue	52 K9
Ratho Close	50 C7	Skibo Court	52 K8
Ravenswood Drive	51 E8	Solway Place	51 E7
Redpath Loan	47 G2	Somerville Way	47 G5
Reid Place	51 G7	Sorn Green	52 J11
Rhynie Road	47 F2	South Parks Road	50 D6
Rimble Loan	51 G7	South Parks Road	51 E7
Rimble Path	51 G7	South Street	53 G7
Rimble Square	51 G7	South Street East	46 D5
Rimbleton	51 G7, G8	South Street West	46 C5
Avenue		Spence Drive	46 B5
Rimbleton Park	51 G7	Stanley Gardens	52 K11
Rimbleton Strip	51 G7	Steadings, The	48 H2
Rimsdale Crescent	47 H2	Stenton Road	51 G9
Rockfield Gardens	47 F2	Stevenson Avenue	51 G6
Rona Place	48 H3	Stirling Road	50 D11
Rosebank Terrace	46 B6	Stob Cross Road	49 M3
Rosebine Court	53 P9	Strathallan Close	52 K11
Rosebine Gardens	53 P9	Strathburn Drive	52 H11
Rosemount Crescent	50 C7	Strathconon Close	48 K3
Rosemount Road	50 B7	Strathdon Park	47 F2
Rothes Park	46 B5	Strathenry Place	46 B6
Rothes Place	46 B5	Strathnairn Court	48 K3
Rothes Road	53 G6	Strathyre Place	48 K2
Rothesay Path	52 J7	Striven Place	51 F7
Rothesay Place	53 H6	Stroma Way	48 H4
Rowallan Green	52 J11	Stuart Road	51 H7
Rowantree Path (1)	52 L7	Sunart Place	51 F7
Roxburgh Road	47 E5	Swan Place	51 G6
Russell Drive	52 J7	Sweetbank Crescent	49 M6
Rutherford Road	51 E10	Sweetbank Drive	49 M5
Ruthven Green	52 K10	Sweetbank Terrace	49 M5
Ryan Road	51 F7	Sythrum Crescent	52 L7
St Drostan Road	52 J7	Talisman Place	50 D8
St Drostans Court	49 N4	Tanna Drive	47 G2
St Regulu's Gardens	52 J7	Tanshall Road East	51 E7
St Ronan's Court	50 D8	Tanshall Road West	50 D8
St Rule Place	52 J7	Tantallon Avenue	52 K9
St Rule Road	52 J7	Tantallon Court	52 K9
St Serf Road	52 J7	Taransay Park	48 H3
Saltire House	51 G8	Taransay Road	48 H4
Sandray Park	47 H3	Tarbert Place	51 F7

Tarland Knowe	47 F3	Whinnyknowe	
Tarves Place	47 F3	Whitecraigs Road	50
Tarvit Green	52 K10	Whitehill Road	
Tay Court	51 F7	Whitworth Road	5
Taylor Drive	52 J8	William Path	
Taylor Gardens	52 J8	Willow Crescent	
Telford Road	52 L8	Wilmington Drive	
Telford Road	53 M8	Woodburn Road	5
Templehall Road	50 D8	Woodgate Drive	
Tern Court	47 G2	Woodgate Way North	
Tern Path	47 G2	Woodgate Way South	
Thane Road	52 J7	Woodlea Grove	
Thistle Drive	47 G3	Woodmill Road	
Thornhill Court	47 E5	Woods Drive	
Tiel Path	52 L7	Woods Place	
Tinnisburn Close	48 K3	Woods Way	
Tofthill Drive	48 L2, L3	Woodside Road	52 J
Tomintoul Place	50 D7	Woodside Walk	
Torphins Avenue	47 F2	Woodside Way	52
Torridon Place	51 F7	Woodstock Court	
Torwood Way	48 K3		
Treaton Place	53 P9		
Tummel Road	48 K3	**Index to Inverkeithing,**	
Turriff Brae	47 F3	**Charlestown, Limekiln**	
Tweedsmuir Court	47 E4	**Rosyth**	
Tyrie Crescent	52 L7		
Uist Road	48 H4	Abbot Place	
Unicorn Gate	53 H6	Aberlour Street	
Unicorn Square	53 H7	Academy Square	
Unicorn Way	53 H7	Admiralty Road	
Union Street	49 N5	Admiralty Road	
Urquhart Green	52 K11	Admiralty Road	
Valley Drive	46 C6	Agnes Paterson	
Valley Gardens	46 C6	Wynd	
Valley Grove	46 C6	Albert Street	
Vardon Drive	52 J8	Alexander Place	
Victoria Path	48 J4	Alma Street	
Victoria Road	49 N6	Anderson Lane	
Viewbank	46 B6	Annabel Court	
Viewfield	51 E9, H9	Aquarius Court	
Viewforth	48 L3	Arrol House	
Walkerton Drive	46 A6	Back o'Yards	
Warout Brae	52 J8	Backmarch Crescent	
Warout Gardens	52 H7	Backmarch Road	
Warout Road	52 H8	Ballast Bank	
Warout Walk	52 H8	Bank Street	
Waverley Court	50 D8	Bannerman Avenue	
Waverley Drive	50 D8	Barham Road	
Well Crescent	52 L8	Barton Road	
Well Gardens	52 L8	Battery Road	5
Well Road	52 K8	Bell Road	
Wellbank Gardens	52 J11	Bevan Place	
Wellesley Path	48 J4	Binning Road	
Wellpark Terrace	49 N5	Blackwood Green	
Wemyss Court	52 K10	Booth Avenue	
West Park Avenue	46 B6	Boreland Park	
Westerlea	46 B5	Boreland Road	
Western Avenue	47 G4, H3	Boyle Drive	
Westgate	46 A5	Brae, The	
Westlaw Place	50 D10	Brankholm Brae	
Westlaw Road	50 D10	Brankholm Crescent	
Westwood Court	53 M7	Brankholm Lane	
Westwood Road	52 L7	Bridge View	
Wheatstone Place	50 D10	Brock Street	

ehaven Crescent	21 E4	Commercial Road	55 Q5	Friary Court	55 Q5
ehaven Road	20 D4	Commodores Walk	56 J6	Furniss Avenue	54 K2
igh Crescent	55 Q4	Communications	54 K1	George Square	55 N1
ey Place	54 L3	House		Gillway	54 J3
side Crescent	55 N2	Concorde Way	55 R4	Glebe Park	57 P6
side Place	55 N3	Covenanters Rise	54 L1	Glebe Terrace	57 P6
side Street	55 N2	Craig Street	55 N3	Globe Road	54 K5
s, The	54 J2	Craig, The	54 K5	Gordon Road	21 H5
s, The	20 A3	Crescent House	54 L1	Grampian Court	54 L5
wells Court	55 R5	Crescent, The	56 H6	Grampian Place	56 L6
lonia Court	54 K1	Cromwell Road	54 M2	Grampian Road	54 L5
lonia Heights	54 K4	Cross Row	20 B3	Grange Road	54 J1
lonia House	54 K5	Crossroads Place	54 M3	Granville Way	54 L4
lonia Road	56 G6	Cruickness Road	57 P7	Gray Place	55 Q4
lonia Way	21 G4	Cult Ness	54 K4	Grayfriar's Walk	55 Q4
pe Road	56 H6	Cunningham Road	54 K5	Great Michael	56 H6, H7
n MacDonald	54 L4	Dales Farm Cottages	55 Q2	Road	
rt		Dales Steading	55 R1	Greig Court	55 P5
lean Crescent	54 K3	Daniel Place	54 J2	Greig Road	21 H5
lean Lane	54 K2	Davenport Place	54 M4	Halketshall	20 C4
eron Grove	55 P4	Deas Road	55 P5	Hall Row	20 B3
erdown Road	56 J6	Dew Way	56 K6	Hamilton Place	54 L3
e Place	54 L4	Dewar House	54 L1	Hamilton Terrace	55 Q5
rnaum Court (1)	20 D4	Dick Place	54 L2	Harbour Place	55 Q5
gnose Court (1)	57 Q9	Double Row	20 B3	Harley Street	55 N3
gnose Park	57 Q9	Douglas Road	54 J5	Haven's Edge	21 E4
gnose Point	57 Q9	Dovecot Wynd	54 M1	Heath Road	54 M4
gnose View	57 Q9	Duffy Place	54 L4	Helen Lane	57 Q9
gnose Way	57 Q9	Dundas House	56 K6	Helen Place	57 Q10
gnose Wynd	57 Q9	Dundas Road	56 K7	Heriot Street	55 Q5
n Place	54 J2	Dundonald Road	54 J4	High Street	55 P5
andhill Cottages	55 N5	Dunfermline Road	21 E4	Hill Street	55 P5
andhill Farm	54 M5	Dunfermline Wynd	55 N5	Hillbank	55 P4
dings		East Bay	57 Q10	Hillend Road	55 R4
andhill Road	55 N5	East Harbour Road	20 B4	Hillfield Crescent	55 P5
e Brae	54 M1	Echobank	55 P5	Hillfield Road	55 P5
e Court	54 M1	Eglinton Place	55 R5	Hillside Camp Road	56 L6
e View	54 M1	Elder Place	54 L2	Hillwood Terrace	55 N4
e Drive	54 L1	Enterprise Way	54 L1	Hilton Cottages	21 G4
e Riggs	55 N1	Esmonde Court	54 L5	Hilton Court	54 K5
e Road	54 J5, L4	Estantia House	54 K1	Hilton Farm	21 H4
el Place	55 Q4	Fair Place	55 P5	Steadings	
erkeithing)		Fairykirk Road	55 N4	Hilton Road	21 G4
el Place (2)	57 Q10	Ferry Lane	57 P9	Hilton Road	54 J5
Queensferry)		Ferry Road	57 P9	Hilton Wynd	54 K5
es Court	21 F4	Ferry Toll Place	56 L6	Holborn Place	54 M2
es Logan Place	54 M3	Ferry Toll Road	54 K5	Hood Place	54 L5
es Way South	21 E4	Ferry Toll Road	56 L6, N7	Hope Street	57 P6
es Way	21 E4	Ferrybarns Court	57 P9	Hopetoun Road	56 K6
ch Lane	20 D4	Ferryhills Road	57 P7	Houliston Avenue	55 P4
ch Road	20 D4	Ferryhills Road	57 Q9	Howe Ness	54 K4
ch Street	20 D4	Fife Place	21 H5	Hudson Road	54 M4
ekilns)		Findlay Crescent	54 L3	Innova Way	56 K6
ch Street	55 Q4	Findlay Street	54 L3	James Miller Road	54 L5
erkeithing)		Foot Place	54 L4	Johnston Park	55 P5
chill Place	54 M4	Forbes Road	54 J5	Jubilee Drive	21 H5
Road	55 P5	Fordell Way	55 R5	Jubilee Drive	56 H6
hore House	54 L1	Forker Avenue	54 J3	Jutland Street	54 K1
land Drive	55 P5	Forsyth House	54 K5	Keith Place	55 Q4
, The	56 K6	Forth Road	21 H5	Keith Road	21 H5
ane Avenue	55 R5	Forth View	55 P5	Keith Road	56 J6
ane Road	56 H6	Forthview House	54 J5	King James IV Road	56 J6
nando Access	56 J6	Forthside Terrace	57 Q10	King Street	55 Q5
		Fraser Avenue	55 R5	King's Crescent	54 L3

King's Place	54 L3
King's Road	54 L3
Kinnell Road	55 P5
Kirkgate	55 P3
Laurel Road	54 J5
Leslie Road	54 M2
Limekilns Road	21 F2
Limpet Ness	54 K4
Linton Place	54 L4
Livesay Road	56 K6
Lochaber	20 B3
Lochinvar Road	56 J6
Lock Road	56 H7
Lothian Court	55 R5
Lothians View	55 N5
Lowry Place	54 M3
McAdam Place	54 L3
McGrigor House (2)	54 K5
McGrigor Road	54 K5
McLean House	54 K1
Main Road	20 B3
(Charlestown)	
Main Road	57 P9
(N Queensferry)	
Main Street	20 C4
(Limekilns)	
Main Street	57 Q10
(N Queensferry)	
Maitland Road	56 G7
Maltings, The	55 Q4
Manse Place	55 P5
Manse Road	55 P5
Masterton Cottages	55 N1
Masterton Road	55 N1
Maxton Place	54 L4
Mellor Court	54 L3
Merlin Drive	55 N1
Middlebank Street	54 M2
Middle Jetty Road	56 H6
Millenium Avenue	56 J6
Milne Road	56 L6
Mitchell Road	56 J6
Mitchell Walk	54 M4
Morris Court	55 Q5
Mossbank	54 M2
Mountbatten Place	54 L4
Mount Hooly	57 Q9
Crescent	
Muckle Hill Park	55 N5
Murray Road	56 K6
Mylneburn	20 D4
Gardens (2)	
Napier Road	56 J6
Nasmyth Road	21 H5
Nelson Street	54 L2
Newton Crescent	55 N3
Newton Place	54 M3
Niven Road	55 Q4
No 1 Dock Road	56 H6
East	
No 1 Dock Road	56 H6
West	
No 2 Dock Road	56 H6
West	

INDEX TO INVERKEITHING & KIRKCALDY

Normandy Place 54 L5
North Esk Road 54 J5
North Loanhead 21 E4
North Road 55 Q3
North Roundall 21 E4
North Row 20 B3
Norval Place 54 M3
Old Kirk Road 57 Q9
Old Orchard, The 20 D4
Orchardhead Way 56 K6
Orchard Square (3) 20 D4
Overhaven 21 E4
Park Lea 55 N2
Park Road 54 L2
Park Road 55 N3
Park Road West 54 K2
Park View Terrace 55 P5
Parkgate 54 M3
Parkside Square 55 N3
Parkside Street 54 M3
Peasehill Brae 54 K4
Peasehill Fauld 54 K5
Peasehill Gait 54 K4
Peasehill Road 54 K4
Penguin House 55 N1
Pier Head Buildings 57 Q10
Pinkerton Place 54 M2
Pitreavie Court 54 K1
Pitreavie Drive 54 K1
Pitreavie Way 54 K1
Port Laing Wynd 57 Q8
Port Street 55 Q5
Post Office 57 Q10
Lane (1)
Preston Crescent 55 Q5
Preston Terrace 57 R6
Primrose Avenue 54 K2
Primrose Court 54 K2
Primrose Lane 54 J2
Primrose Road 21 H3
Promenade 20 C4
Queen Margaret's 57 Q9
Place
Queen Mary 55 P5
Terrace
Queen Street 55 P5
Queen's Buildings 54 L3
Queens Way 21 H5
Queensferry 54 L1
House
Queensferry 54 L2, M3
Road
Ramsay Lane 20 D4
Ramsey Place 54 M4
Rannoch Road 54 L5
Red Row 20 D4
Ridley Drive 54 M4
Rocks Road 20 B3
Roman Road 55 P5
Romyn Road 56 J6
Roods Crescent 55 P4
Roods Road 55 P5
Roods Square 55 P4
Ropeway 56 H6

St John's Court 55 R4
St Margaret's 54 K5
House (1)
St Peter's Court 55 R4
Saltpans 20 B3
Salvage Road 56 H6
Sandilands 20 D4
Scotmill Way 55 Q4
Selkirk Road 56 H7
Selvage Place 55 N4
Selvage Street 55 N4
Shamrock Terrace 57 P7
Sherbrooke Road 54 K5
Shinwell Place 54 L4
Signal Station 57 Q10
Skylark Road 55 N1
Somerville Court 55 Q4
Somerville Road 54 J5
South Castle Drive 54 M1
South Loanhead 21 E4
South Roundall 21 E4
South Row 20 B3
Spencerfield Road 55 R5
Spens Lane 56 J6
Spittalfield Crescent 55 Q5
Spittalfield Road 55 Q5
Stables Road 56 J6
Stephen's Drive 55 Q4
Struan Drive 55 P4
Struan Place 55 P4
Stuart Road 55 J5
Syme Place 54 J2
Thomson House 54 K1
Thomson Place 54 M4
Torridon Drive 54 L5
Torridon Lane 54 L5
Torridon Place 54 L5
Tovey Road 54 K5
Townhall Street 55 Q5
Train Terrace 54 J2
Tyrwhitt Place 54 M4
Upper Wellheads 21 E4
Viking Way 54 K5
Waggon Road 20 D1
Waggon Road 55 Q5
Walter Hay Court 54 M4
Warrington Court 20 D4
Watt Road 21 H5
Webster Place 54 J2
Well Lane 21 E4
Welldean Cottages 57 N8
Wellheads, The 20 D4
Wemyss Court 54 L2
Wemyss Street 54 L2
West Harbour 20 A3
Road
West Road 20 A3
Wester Gellet 21 G1
Farm Cottages
Whinneyknowe 57 Q9
Whinny Hill 57 N6
Crescent
Whinnyburn Place 54 K2
Wilson Way 54 K5

Wood Place 54 L2
Wood Road 21 H5
Wood Road 54 J5
Woodlands, The 54 M2
Woodside Avenue 54 L2
Woodside Street 54 M2
Zealandia Road 56 H6

Index to Kirkcaldy

Abbots Mill 71 F8
Abbots Walk 70 E8
Abbotshall Road 71 F8
Aboyne Gardens 66 D3
Adam Smith Court 71 H7
Adam Smith's Close 71 H7
Adamson Avenue 67 G5
Ailsa Grove 67 E3
Aitken Court 71 G9
Aitken Street 69 K4
Alexander Street 69 M4
Alexandra Street 71 H6
Alford Avenue 66 D4
Alison Street 71 G9
Allardice Crescent 70 C6
Alloway Drive 67 F4
Almond Place 68 H3
Anderson Street (2) 69 M4
Anderson Street 69 K5
Annsmuir Place 67 E2
Appin Crescent 66 D4
Arran Crescent 67 E4
Ashludie Place 67 E1
Asquith Street 71 F8
Atholl Terrace 66 C4
Ava Street 71 F9
Aytoun Avenue 66 C2
Balcomie Road 67 E1
Baldwin Crescent 71 F6
Balfour Street 71 G6
Balmoral Drive 70 C6
Balsusney Road 71 G6
Balwearie Crescent 71 F9
Balwearie Gardens 70 E10
Balwearie Road 71 F9
Bandon Avenue 69 L3
Bank Street 69 K4
Barassie Drive 67 E2
Barclay Court 68 J2
Barnet Crescent 71 G10
Barnton Road 67 E1
Barry Road 67 E2
Beatty Court 68 J4
Beatty Crescent 68 J3
Beatty Crescent 68 J4
Beaufort Crescent 70 C6
Beauly Place 66 D4
Begg Road 66 B2
Bell Inn Wynd (1) 71 H8
Belleisle Road 68 F1
Ben Alder Place 70 D6
Ben Ledi Road 70 E6
Ben Nevis Place 70 E6

Benarty Street 7
Bennochy Avenue 7
Bennochy Court 7
Bennochy Gardens 7
Bennochy Grove 7
Bennochy Park 7
Bennochy Road 6
Bennochy Road 71 F6
Bennochy View 7
Berwick Place 7
Berwick Place 6
Bethelfield Place (5) 7
Beveridge Road 6
Biggin Wa's 6
Binney Wells 6
Birnam Road 6
Birrell Close (3) 6
Birrell Street 6
Wynd (2) 6
Birrells Lane 6
Blackcraigs 6
Blair Place 7
Blairmore Road 6
Blyth Gardens 6
Blyth Street 6
Bogies Wynd 6
Boglily Road 7
Boreland Place 6
Boreland Road 6
Bowhouse Drive 70
Bowhouse Gardens 70
Braehead Cottages
Braehead House
Braehead Road 6
Braids Road 6
Branning Court (5) 6
Branxton Wynd 70
Briarcliffe Street 6
Bridge Street 71
Broad Wynd 6
Brodick Road 6
Broom Gardens 6
Broom Place 6
Broom Road 6
Broomside 6
Buchanan Court 6
Bute Wynd 6
Cairngorm Crescent 6
Cairns Street East 6
Cairns Street West 6
Cairnwell Place 6
Caithness Court 6
Caithness Place 6
Cameron Drive 6
Caledonia Road 7
Calender Avenue 6
Camperdown Place 6
Campsie Crescent 6
Canmore Gardens 6
Canon Byrne Glebe 6
Carberry Place 6
Carberry Road 6
Carlyle Road 6
Carnethy Crescent 6

dale Gardens	67 E2	Den Road	68 H5	Forth Park Drive	71 F6	Huntly Crescent	66 B3
n Place	66 C2	Denburn Place	68 H5	Forth Park Gardens	71 F6	Hutchison Way	66 C2
hinny	69 K2	Denburn Road	68 J4	Forth View	71 G10	Inch View	70 G12
emount Terrace	66 B3	Denend Crescent	67 G5	Fountain View	67 H2	Inchgarvie Road	67 E3
lor Crescent	66 D4	Denfield Place	68 J4	Frances Row	69 M1	Inchkeith Crescent	70 G13
on Place	69 K2	Doctor's Row	69 L3	Frances View	69 M3	Institution Street	69 K4
iana's	71 G6	Dollar Crescent	66 C4	Fraser Place	69 M3	Invertiel Bank	71 G10
ace (1)		Dornoch Crescent	66 D2	Frederick Wilson	68 F4	Invertiel Road	70 F11
r Avenue	68 H4	Dothan Cottages	66 A1	Park		Invertiel Terrace	71 G10
r House	68 G3	Douglas Street	71 G8	Gas Wynd	71 G9	Iona House	66 B2
el Grove	66 B3	Dovecot Crescent	69 M3	George Burn Wynd	71 H8	Ivy Lane	69 M4
el Level	66 C2	Downfield Place	68 F1	George Street	71 G8	James Grove	71 G9
el Park	66 B2	Dronachy Road	70 E7	Gillespie Grove	66 C1	Jawbanes Road	70 F12
el Place	66 B2	Duddingston Drive	67 E1	Gladney Square	71 G9	Jean Armour	67 E3
el Road	66 B3	Dunbar Place	70 D6	Glamis Road	66 C4	Gardens	
elhill	66 C3	Duncan Street	71 F7	Glasswork Street	71 G8	John Street	71 G6
elton Drive	66 B2	Dunearn Drive	67 E5	Glebe Park	71 H6	John Hunter Court	71 G7
otte Street	71 G8	Dunnikier Road	68 G4	Glen Albyn Drive	66 A2	John Paul Jones	66 C1
tnut Avenue	68 H4	Dunnikier Road	71 H6	Glen Bruar Place	66 A3	Court	
ot Road	67 E4	Dunnikier Way	68 G3	Glen Clova Place	66 B2	Johnny Marshall's	68 F2
's Close (4)	68 J5	Dunnikier Way	69 K2	Glen Esk Place	66 A2	Loan	
ie Place	68 J4	Dunnottar Place	70 D7	Glen Isla Road	66 B3	Junction Road	68 J5
ch Court	71 H7	Dunrobin Road	70 D7	Glen Lyon Road	66 A2	Jute Place	68 H4
ch Lane	71 H7	Dunsire Street	69 K3	Glen More Gardens	66 A2	Katherine Park	67 G5
ch Street	69 K5	Dunure Place	70 D7	Glen Roy Place	66 A2	Katherine Street	67 G5
a Glebe (1)	68 J5	Dunvegan Avenue	70 C6	Glenbervie Road	67 E2	Katrine Crescent	66 D3
Place	71 F6	Dysart Road	69 K5	Glendale Park	66 A2	Kelso Place	67 G5
n Gardens	67 E5	Earn Road	68 J3	Glendevon Place	67 E2	Kenmore Terrace	66 D4
iden Place	71 F8	East Albert Road	71 H6	Gleneagles Gardens	68 F2	Kennedy Crescent	67 F5
Court	66 B2	East Burn Court	68 J4	Gosford Road	66 B5	Kidd Street	68 J4
Wynd	71 H7	East Fergus Place	71 G8	Gourlay Street	71 F7	Kilgour Avenue	68 J4
mercial Street	68 J5	East March Street	69 K4	Gow Crescent	71 G7	Kilmun Road	66 C4
Place	69 M3	East Port	69 M4	Grampian Gardens	70 E6	Kilspindie Crescent	68 F2
Street	69 M3	East Quality Street	69 M4	Greenloanings	66 C3	King Street	67 F5
n Street	71 H8	East Vows Walk	70 G12	Grieve Street	67 F5	Kinghorn Road	70 G11
House	66 A3	Edington Place	69 N3	Gullane Place	67 E1	Kinghorn Road	70 F13
earn Avenue	66 A4	Edward Street	68 G4	Haig Avenue	68 J4	Kininmonth Street	71 G9
earn Place	66 B4	Edzell Park	67 E2	Halleys Court	71 G9	Kinnaird Place	70 C7
foot Court	70 G13	Elgin House	67 G5	Hallows, The	69 L3	Kirk Wynd	71 G7
foot Place	70 G12	Elgin Street	67 G5	Harcourt Road	71 G6	Kyles, The	69 K5
foot Walk	70 G12	Ellisland Avenue	67 E4	Harriet Street	69 K5	Laburnum Drive	68 H3
e Place	68 F1	Ellon Road	66 B3	Harris Drive	67 E3	Lady Helen Street	71 G9
evar Gardens	70 D6	Elm Place	70 E6	Hawksmuir	68 J5	Lady Inn Wynd (2)	71 G8
mount	66 C4	Esplanade	71 G10, H7	Hayfield Place	68 F4	Lady Nairn Avenue	69 K5
ond Gardens	67 E4	Ettrick Drive	67 E4	Hayfield Road	68 F4, J4	Lakeside Road	70 E7
ord Court	71 F8	Factory Road	68 J5	Hazel Avenue	67 G5	Lammermuir Place	70 E6
arty Place	69 K4	Fair Isle Road	66 D3	Heggie's Wynd	71 G10	Lansbury Street	69 K4
n Crescent	69 M4	Fairway, The	69 L3	Hendry Crescent	67 F5	Larrach Court	66 B3
n Crescent	66 D4	Falkland View	69 L2	Hendry Road	67 F3	Lauder Road	67 G5
an Crescent	66 B4	Fallodon Crescent	71 F8	Hendry's Wynd	71 G9	Laurel Crescent	67 F5
rae Court	67 F3	Farne Court	67 E3	Heron Place	66 D1	Lawson Gardens	69 K3
rae Terrace	67 E3	Fergus Wynd	71 G10	Hie Gait (7)	69 M5	Lawson Street	69 K3
s Drive	66 D4	Ferrard Road	71 F7	High Street (Dysart)	69 M4	Legion Court	71 F6
ahoy Crescent	68 F2	Findhorn Place	66 D3	High Street (Kirkcaldy)	71 G8	Leslie Street	70 F11
ar Drive	66 D3	Fish Wynd	71 H6	Hill Place	71 H7	Liberton Road	67 E2
Street	71 G8	Fitzroy Square	69 M4	Hill Street (Dysart)	69 M4	Lilac Crescent	68 H4
Park Brae	66 B2	Fitzroy Street	69 M4	Hill Street (Kirkcaldy)	71 G8	Lina Street	71 G6
Park Court	66 A2	Flesh Wynd	68 J5	Hillcrest Avenue	66 D5	Lindores Drive	66 C3
Park Drive	66 A2	Fleming Drive	66 D2	Holly Place	68 H4	Links Street	71 G10
Park Gardens	66 A2	Floors Place	70 C6	Hopetoun Place	66 B5	Linn Place	68 F1
Park Grove	66 B2	Forbes Terrace (3)	71 G6	Hot Pot Wynd	69 M5	Linton Lane	66 D5
Park Way	66 B2	Fordell Gardens	70 C6	Howard Place	69 M4	Linum Grove	68 H4
Road	71 F7	Forres Drive	66 B4	Hunter Place	71 G8	Lismore Avenue	67 E4
Wharf	71 H7	Forth Avenue	71 F7	Hunter Street	71 G8	Lismore Place	67 E4

Street	Ref	Street	Ref	Street	Ref	Street	Ref
Little Lane (4)	71 G8	Morven Grove	67 E4	Portland Gardens	67 E2	Saladin Street	
Loanhead Place	71 F6	Muirfield Court	68 J1	Postings, The	71 G8	Salisbury Street	7
Lochlea Grove	68 F4	Muirfield Street	68 F2	Pottery Street	69 K2	Sandwell Crescent	70
Lockhart Lane	66 C1	Muirhead	68 J1	Powfoot Road	67 E1	Sang Place	7
Lomond Gardens	70 E6	Munro Street	71 G9	Pratt Street	71 F9	Sang Road	7
lONG bRAES	71 f7	Murray Terrace (2)	71 G6	Prestonfield Drive	67 E2	Sauchenbush Road	7
Long Craig Walk	70 G11	Muttonhall Cottages	67 E3	Prestwick Place	67 E2	Saunders Court	7
Longbraes Gardens	66 C5	Myregormie Place	69 K2	Prime Gilt Box Street	67 G5	Saunders Street	71
Loom Road	67 G5	Myrtle Crescent	68 F4	Provost Kay Park	67 H5	Saut Girnal	6
Lord Gambier Wharf	71 H7	Nairn Street	68 J5	Purves Court	71 G9	Wynd (6)	
Lorne Street	69 K4	Napier Street	69 K3	Quality Street	69 M4	School Brae	6
Lothian Terrace	68 F4	Nelson Street	67 G5	Quarry Brae	69 L3	School Lane	
Loughborough	69 L4	Nether Street	71 J6	Race Road	69 L1	School Wynd	7
Road		Nether Street	69 N4	Raeburn Crescent	71 F7	Scotscraig Place	6
McDouall Stuart	69 M4	New Row	69 M2	Raith Crescent	71 F7	Scott Street	7
Place (5)		Newliston Drive	66 B4	Raith Drive	71 F8	Seafield Court	7C
MacIndoe Crescent	68 J3	Newtonmore Drive	67 E2	Raith Gardens	71 F8	Seafield Crescent	7C
McIntosh Court	66 D2	Nicol Street	71 G8	Ralston Drive	67 E2	Seafield Gardens	7C
McIntosh Gardens	66 D2	Nile Street	67 G5	Ramsay Road	71 G10	Seafield Road	7C
McIntosh Parade	66 D2	Normand Brae	69 M4	Randolph Court	69 M3	Seafield View	7C
McIntosh Park	66 D2	Normand Road	69 M4	Randolph Crescent	69 M1	Seaforth Place	
McIntosh Place	66 D2	North Fergus Place	71 G8	Randolph Place	69 M2	Seton Place	6
McKenzie Street	69 K4	Novar Crescent	71 G9	Randolph Road	69 L2	Shepherd Street	6
Malcolms Meadow	66 D2	Oaktree Court	68 H3	Ranfurly Gardens	67 E2	Shetland Place	6
Malcolm's Wynd	71 H6	Oaktree Square	68 H3	Rannoch Road	66 D3	Shore Road	6
Maltings Road	68 J4	Ochil Avenue	70 E6	Ratho Place	67 E1	Sidlaw Street	6
Maple Street	68 G4	Octavia Street	71 G6	Ravens Craig	69 K5	Sir Thomas Elder	6
Maree Place	66 D2	Oliphant Way	66 D1	Ravenscraig Street	69 K5	Court	
Maria Street	71 H6	Ollerton Court	71 G6	Rectory Lane	69 M4	Sir Thomas Elder	6
Mariners Street	67 G5	Olympia Arcade	71 G8	Redburn Wynd	71 H7	Way	
Marion Street	71 G9	Orchard Lane (4)	69 M4	Redcraigs	66 B4	Skibo Place	7
Marjory's Avenue	66 C2	Orchard Place (1)	69 M4	Regent Place	71 G6	Smeaton Gardens	6
Maryhall Street	71 H6	Oriel Crescent	71 F7	Rev Shirra Street	66 C2	Smeaton Road	7
Marywell	71 H6	Oriel Road	66 C5	Riverview	70 G11	Smith's Terrace	7
Massereene Road	70 E6	Oriel Road	71 F7	Robert Adam Drive	66 C2	South Fergus Place	7
Matthew Street	67 G5	Orkney Place	69 K4	Robert Philip Road	66 D2	South Row	6
Mauchline Grove	67 F3	Ostlere Road	71 F7	Roberts Street	69 K3	Southerton Crescent	
Meikle Square (3)	69 M4	Oswald Court	69 L2	Roomlin Gardens	69 L4	Southerton Gardens	
Meikle Loan	66 D1	Oswald Road	69 K2	Rosabelle Street	69 K4	Southerton Road	
Meldrum Court	71 G6	Oswalds Wynd	71 H7	Rose Wynd (3)	71 G8	Spencer Place	7
Meldrum Road	71 G6	Otterston Place	66 D3	Roseberry Court	71 G6	Spey Avenue	6
Mellerstain Road	66 B5	Overton Court	69 K3	Roseberry Terrace	71 G6	Stanley Park	7
Melrose Crescent	68 H5	Overton Mains	68 J3	Rosemount Avenue	67 F3	Station Court	7
Melville Place	70 C6	Overton Road	68 J3	Rosin Court	68 H4	Station Road	6
Menzies Crescent	70 E6	Pan Ha'	69 M5	Ross Gardens	69 K4	(Dysart)	
Merchant Place	69 K1	Panmure Place	67 E1	Rosslyn Gardens	69 L2	Station Road	7
Methven Place	71 G9	Pannie Road	68 J4	Rosslyn Street	69 L1, L3	(Kirkcaldy)	
Methven Road	71 G9	Park Place	71 G8	Rowan House	68 G3	Stewart Street	6
Michael Nairn	66 D2	Park Road	69 K2	Russell Place	71 H6	Stobs Place	6
Gardens		Park View	67 E5	Rutherford Court	69 K4	Stocks Street	6
Michael Nairn Grove	66 D2	Path, The	71 J6	Rymalton	68 J5	Strathallan Drive	6
Michael Nairn Parade	66 D2	Pathhead Court	68 J5	St Brycedale Avenue	71 G7	Strathkinnes Road	6
Michael Nairn Park	66 D2	Patterson Place	67 G5	St Brycedale Court	71 G7	Striven Place	6
Mid Street	68 J5	Patterson Street	67 G5	St Brycedale Road	71 G7	Sutherland Place	6
Midfield Road	68 J1	Peebles Street	70 G11	St Clair Street	69 K4	Swan Road	6
Mill Street	71 F10	Pentland Place	67 E5	St Clair Terrace	69 M2	Sycamore Avenue	6
Miller Street	69 L3	Percival Street	71 F6	St Fillans Place	66 C4	Tarbolton Court	6
Millie Street	68 J5	Pitcairn Place	66 D1	St Fillans Road	66 C4	Tay Place	7
Milton Road	71 G9	Pitfour Place	66 B4	St Kilda Crescent	67 E3	Templehall	7
Minto Place	70 E7	Pitreavie Place	67 E1	St Mary's Glebe	71 H6	Avenue	
Mitchell Place	68 J5	Pool Lane	69 L2	St Mary's Place	71 H6	Terrace Street	7
Mitchell Street	71 H7	Poplar Crescent	68 F4	St Mary's Road	71 H6	Thistle Street	7
Mitchelston Drive	69 K1	Poplar Gardens	68 F4	St Serfs Place	69 M4	Thornhill Drive	6
Montgomery Street	71 G6	Port Brae	71 H7	Sailors' Walk	69 M5	Thornhill Drive	6

Place	67 E3	William Sinclair	66 C1	Blackwood Place	75 J5
oth Street	71 H8	Street		Bonthron Lane (1)	80 D12
ain Road	66 A5	Williams Grove	68 H2	Bourtree Bank	74 E7
ain	66 C3	Williamson's Quay	71 H7	Bow Street	81 E10
ain Place	68 F1	Willow Drive	68 G4	Bowhouse Place	80 D8
ion Place	66 D3	Wilson Avenue	67 F5	Bowling Green	81 G8
nham Court	69 M4	Windmill Green	69 L3	Street	
r Terrace	69 L3	Windmill Place	69 M3	Brady Crescent	81 E9
head	69 M4	Windmill Road	69 L3	Braehead Gardens	80 D11
send Crescent	71 H7	Windygate	70 E9	Braeside	81 G8
send Place	71 G7	Winifred Crescent	67 F5	Branch Street	75 J6
nel Drive	66 C3	Winifred Street	67 F5	Brewery Wynd	75 J6
erry Drive	68 F2	Wishart Place	69 L5	Bridge Street	75 H6
f Place	66 D3	Woodlands Road	66 C5	Broom Crescent	75 H4
d Avenue	69 K3	Woodlands Walk	68 H3	Broom Road	75 H4
rum Place	66 D4	Yetholm Way	68 H5	Broomie Knowe	75 H6
Avenue	70 G12	York Place	69 L2	Brown Crescent	80 D8
Court	70 G12	Young's Terrace	71 H6	Brown Street	80 D11
Farm	70 G12			Buchan Gardens	80 D10
ages				Burnmill Road	75 H6
Gardens	70 G12	**Index to Leven, Innerleven,**		Burns Avenue	80 D11
Grove	70 G12	**Methil & Buckhaven**		Byron Street	81 E8
Street	69 L4			Cairns Terrace	80 D8
hart Court	70 C6	Abbie Grove	74 E6	Carberry Court	75 K5
y Gardens	67 E5	Adamson Terrace	75 H5	Carberry Park	75 K5
th		Addison Crescent	74 G5	Carberry Road	75 K5
Gardens	67 E5	Aithernie Court	75 H5	Carlow Court	75 H6
View	67 E5	Aithernie Road	75 H5	Carlyle Crescent	80 D11
ica Crescent	68 H3	Aitken Court (3)	75 J6	Carmichael Court (6)	75 J6
oy Street	67 F5	Aitken Street	75 J6	Casan	74 G4
ria Gardens	71 G7	Ajax Way	81 H8	Castle Crescent	74 D3
ria Road	71 G6	Alder Terrace	74 E7	Cedar Avenue	74 D7
ria Street	69 M4	Alexander Street	80 A12	Centenary Court	74 G6
orth Avenue	69 L4	Alison Street	80 D11	Chapel Street	80 D11
orth Gardens	69 L4	Anderson Court	75 J6	Chemiss Road	80 D8
orth Street	69 L4	Anderson Lane	80 D12	Cherry Court	81 E8
orth Terrace	69 L3	Anderson Street	75 J5	Chestnut Avenue	74 D7
teer's Green	71 H8	Arbaile	74 G4	Chestnut Crescent	74 E6
The	69 N4	Ardan	74 G4	Christie Avenue	74 G5
er Street	67 G5	Arnbeg	75 H5	Church Road	75 J5
ry Wynd	71 G10	Ashgrove	80 C8	Church Street	80 D11
Street	69 M4	Ashgrove Court	80 C8	Clyde Street	81 E10
rley Road	69 K2	Baird Crescent	75 J5	Coldstream Avenue	75 J4
ers Crescent	67 G5	Balfour Street	75 K5	Coldstream	75 J4
lerburn Road	66 B4	Balmaise	74 G4	Crescent	
yss Road	69 N3	Balmoral Place	75 J5	Coldstream Park	75 J4
yssfield	71 G7	Balmoral Terrace	75 J5	College Court	80 D11
Albert Road	71 G7	Banbeath Cottages	74 F5	College Street	80 D11
Fergus Place	71 G8	Banbeath Court	74 G5	Commercial Road	75 J6
March Street	68 J4	Banbeath Place	74 G4	Coronation	74 G5
Port	69 M4	Banbeath Road	74 G5	Crescent	
Quality Street	69 M4	Bank Street	75 J6	Cowley Street	81 E9
Torbain	66 C3	Barncraig Street	81 E10	Crown Wynd (12)	75 J6
Vows Walk	70 G12	Barrie Street	81 F8	Cupar Road	75 J3
Wynd	68 J5	Barron Terrace	75 J4	Cypress Lane	75 H3
er Bogie Road	66 A4	Bayview Crescent	81 G8	Daisy Grove	80 C8
wood Avenue	69 K3	Bayview Terrace	75 J6	Dee Street	81 E9
tfield Road	68 J2	Beech Avenue	74 E7	Den Street	81 E10
e Melville Road	71 F7	Beech Park	75 H4	Den Walk	81 F8
ebank Gardens	67 G5	Bethune Way (4)	81 E11	Den Walk	80 D10
ehouse Avenue	71 G8	Beurard	74 G4	Dewar Buildings (2)	75 J6
eman's Brae	68 G3	Birch Grove	74 D7	Dewar Drive	75 H5
escauseway	71 G8	Blacketyside	75 K3	Diadem Place (2)	81 E11
m Street	71 G9	Cottages		Don Street	81 E10

Donaldson Road	74 D7
Dubbieside	75 H7
Dunsire Street	80 D8
Durie Court	81 G8
Durie Lane	74 G4
Durie Street (Methil)	81 G8
Durie Street (Leven)	75 J6
Durward Street	75 J5
Dyke Neuk	75 H4
Eagle Road	80 C10
Earl Haig Avenue	75 H5
East High Street	81 E11
East Links	75 K5
Elmwood Road	74 D7
Erskine Court	81 H8
Erskine Street	81 E11
Factory Road	80 D12
Falcon Road	80 C10
Fisher Street	81 G8
Forest Path	75 H3
Forman Road	75 J6
Forth Street	81 F10
(Buckhaven)	
Forth Street	75 J6
(Leven)	
Gallacher Avenue	75 H5
Gardner Crescent	74 F6
Gillespie Lane (3)	81 E11
Gilmour Avenue	75 H5
Gladstone Street	75 J5
Glebe Street	75 J5
Glen Grove	75 H4
Glenburn	75 H4
Glencairn Crescent	75 H4
Glencairn Gardens	75 J4
Glendale	75 H4
Glenfield Court	81 G8
Glenlyon Place	75 H6
Glenlyon Road	75 H5
Glenthorne Road	75 H7
Graham Avenue	74 F5
Graham Crescent	74 F5
Greengates	75 H4
Greenfield View	74 E5
Grieve Street	80 D8
Groban	74 G4
Grunnan	74 G4
Harbour View	81 H8
Harbour View Road	75 H7
Harbour Wynd	81 G8
Haughgate Avenue	75 J5
Haughgate Street	75 J5
Haughgate Terrace	75 J5
Haven Court	81 G8
Hawkslaw Gardens	75 H6
Hawkslaw Road	75 H6
Hawkslaw Street	75 H6
Hawthorn Street	81 E8
(Methil)	
Hawthorn Street	75 J5
(Leven)	
Hazel Dene	74 D7
Herd Crescent	80 D8
Herriot Crescent	81 G8

Name	Ref	Name	Ref
High Street (Methil)	81 G8	Mallard Road	80 D10
High Street (Leven)	75 J6	Manse Place (Kennoway)	74 D3
Holly Grove	75 H4	Manse Place (Leven)	75 J6
Holly Road	75 H3	Maple Gardens	81 E8
Hollybank	74 D6	Marine Villas	75 K6
Institute Row	80 D8	Martin Street	80 D10
Institution Street	81 E10	Mathieson Place	80 D8
Ivygrove	80 D8	Mavis Bank	80 C10
Janetta Terrace (1)	75 H6	Mavis Court	80 D10
Keir Hardie Street	81 F9	Memorial Court	81 G9
Kenmore Terrace	81 E10	Memorial Road	81 F9
Kennoway Road	74 G4	Merlin Court	80 D10
Kestrel Grove	80 D9	Merlin Crescent	80 D10
Kinghorn Place	81 G8	Methil Brae	74 F7
Kinnarchie Brae	75 H7	Methil Brae	81 G8
Kinnarchie Crescent	75 H7	Methilhaven Road	80 D10
Kinnarchie Park	75 H7	Methilhaven Road	74 G7
Kinnear Street	80 D11	Michael Street	80 D11
Kirke Park	74 D7	Middleton Place	74 G5
Kirkland Drive	81 E8	Midlaw Crescent	74 G5
Kirkland Gardens	74 F7	Millburn Terrace	75 J5
Kirkland Road	81 G8	Mitchell Street	75 J6
Kirkland Villas	74 F7	Montgomery Drive	74 G6
Kirkland Walk	74 D7, F7	Montrave Crescent	75 H5
Kirkside Court	75 J6	Morar Street	81 E8
Knowe, The	74 D3	Mountfleurie Crescent	74 G5
Laburnum Road	74 E7	Mountfleurie Street	74 G5
Lady Wynd	81 E11	Mulberry Court	74 E6
Laird Avenue	81 G8	Myreside Avenue	74 D3
Larchfield	74 E7	Myreside Gardens	74 D3
Largo Road	75 K4	Myreside Place	74 D3
Laurel Avenue	74 D7	Narrow Wynd (13)	75 J6
Lawrence Court	80 D12	Nairn Street	75 J6
Lawrence Drive	74 F5	National Court	81 G9
Lawrence Street	80 D11	North Links	75 K5
Lawrie Terrace	75 H5	North Street	75 J6
Lawson Lane	80 D12	Oakvale Road	74 D7
Leargan	75 H4	Old Inn Wynd	75 J6
Lemon Terrace	75 J5	Old Mill Court	75 H5
Letham Avenue	75 J5	Omar Crescent	80 D11
Letham Terrace	75 J5	Orchard Grove	74 G4
Leven Vale	75 H6	Orchard House	74 G4
Levenbank Drive	74 E6	Ossian Crescent	81 F8
Lilac Bank	74 E7	Oswald Place (7)	75 J6
Lime Grove	74 D7	Page Place	80 D8
Links Lane	75 K6	Page Road	74 D7
Links Place	75 J6	Park Avenue	75 H4
Links Road	75 J6	Park Drive	75 H4
Linksfield Street	75 J6	Parker Terrace	75 H6
Linnwood Drive	74 G4	Parkhill Terrace	75 J6
Linnwood Gardens	75 H4	Parkhill Wynd (5)	75 J6
Lochiel Place	81 E8	Parkhill	75 J6
Logie Street	81 G8	Parkland Court	81 E10
Lomond Gardens	81 E8	Patterson Street	75 H7
Lundin View	75 J3	Percival Road	80 C10
McDonald Street	81 G8	Pirnie Street	80 D8
McDonald Terrace	81 G8	Poplar Road	74 D7
McDuff Street	80 A12	Promenade	75 J6
MacFarlane Court	80 D8	Queens Avenue	80 D8
McIntosh Crescent	74 G5	Queens Square	74 D7
Mackie Avenue	75 H5	Randolph Court	80 D12
Main Avenue	80 A12		
Main Street	80 C8		
Maitland Street	75 J5		

Name	Ref	Name	Ref
Randolph Street	80 D12	Station Place	80
Rannoch Road	81 F8	Station Road (Buckhaven)	80
Raven Crescent	80 D9	Station Road (Methil)	8
Rising Sun Road	81 E11	Station Road) (Leven	7
River Side	75 H6	Stewart Court	8
Riverside Road	75 H6	Summer Road	8C
Riverside Way	74 E6	Suttie Street	8
Robertson Avenue	74 F5	Swallow Crescent	8C
Robin Crescent	80 C10	Swan Court	8
Rose Street	81 H8	Swan Street	8
Rose Terrace	75 J5	Swan View	8
Roseberry Terrace (14)	75 J6	Sycamore Avenue	7
Rosemount Grove	74 F6	Tay Street	81
Rosie Cottages	80 B12	Taylor Street	7
Rowan Crescent	74 E7	Thistle Terrace	7
Rowan Lane	74 E6	Thrush Avenue	8C
Ruskin Crescent	80 D9	Toboggan Road	7
St Andrew Square	81 G8	Toll Avenue	8
Sandwell Street	80 D10	Towers, The	
Sawmill Cottages	80 D11	Trinity Place	
School Lane	75 J6	Turner Crescent	8
School Road	80 D8	Turnstiles, The	8
School Street (Methil)	81 G8	Turpie Road	7
School Street (Leven)	75 J6	Tweed Street	81
School Wynd	75 J6	Union Place (9)	
Scoonie Brae	75 J4	Union Street (8)	
Scoonie Court	75 J4	Union Terrace	8C
Scoonie Crescent	75 J5	Vettriano Vale	
Scoonie Drive	75 J5	Victoria Road (Buckhaven)	8C
Scoonie Park	75 J4	Victoria Road	
Scoonie Place	75 J5	View Forth	
Scoonie Road	75 J5	Viewforth Place	
Scoonie Terrace	75 J4	Viewforth Square (15)	
Sea Road	81 E9	Viewforth	8C
Seagate	75 J6	Waggon Road	
Seaview Lane	80 D11	Wall Street	81
Selkirk Street	81 F8	Walnut Crescent	7
Shakespeare Avenue	80 D11	Walnut Grove	7
Shepherd Avenue	74 F5	Ward Street	81
Shepherd Crescent	74 F5	Water Baulk	8C
Shepherds Park	81 F9	Well Wynd	7
Shore Street	80 D12	Wellesley Court	8
Shorehead (10)	75 J6	Wellesley Road	8C
Shotburn Crescent	75 H5	Wellesley Road	8
Sillerhole Road	75 H4	Wemyss Place	8
Simon Crescent	80 C8	Wemysshaven Gardens	8C
Silverburn Cottages	75 L4	West High Street	8C
Smith Road	74 D7	West Wynd	8C
Smithyhill Cottages	80 B8	Wester Durie Cottages	
Somerville Road	75 H5	Wheatley Street	
South Grove	81 G9	White Avenue	7
South Street (Methil)	81 H8	Whyte Rose Terrace	7
South Street (Leven)	75 J6	William Laing Crescent (4)	
Spey Street	81 E9	Wilkie Cottages	
Springbank Villas	75 K6	Willow Bank	7
Standing Stane Road	80 A9, B8		
Stanmore Place	75 H6		
Stark Street	80 D9		
Station Court	75 H5		

w Glade	75 H3	Churchill Crescent	87 E4	James Street	87 E3	Murray Place	87 E2
n Square	80 D8	City Road	86 D2	Jamie Anderson	87 E5	Murrayfield Road	86 B3
sor Wynd (11)	75 J6	Clatto Place	86 D4	Place		Muttoes Court (2)	87 E2
ygates Road	74 G5	Claybraes	86 D4	John Coupar Court	87 E3	Muttoes Lane (1)	87 E2
lbank Cottages	80 A9	College Street	87 E2	John Knox Road	86 C5	Nelson Street	87 E3
dlands Crescent	74 G4	Condie Court	87 E2	John Street	86 D3	Newmill Gardens	86 C4
Street	80 C10	Crails Lane (3)	87 E2	Johnston Court	87 E2	North Castle Street	87 F2
		Crawford Gardens	86 D4	Kennedy Gardens	86 D2	North Street	87 E2
		David Russell	86 B3	Kidston Court	87 F2	Old Station Road	86 C1
k to St Andrews		Apartments		Kilrymont Crescent	87 F5	Park Street	87 E3
		Dean's Court	87 F2	Kilrymont Place	87 F4	Pends, The	87 F2
y Court	87 F2	Dempster Court	87 E3	Kilrymont Road	87 F4	Pilmour Links	86 D2
y Park	87 F3	Dempster Terrace	87 E3	Kinburn Place	86 D2	Pilmour Place	87 E2
y Street	87 F2	Donaldson Gardens	86 D3	Kinburn Terrace	86 D2	Pipeland Farm	87 E5
y Walk	87 F3	Doocot Road	86 B4	King Street	87 E4	Pipeland Road	87 E4
tsford Crescent	87 E2	Doubledykes Road	86 D2	Kinkell Terrace	87 G4	Pipeland Walk	87 E4
tsford Place	87 E2	Drumcarrow Road	86 D4	Kinness Place	87 E3	Playfair Terrace	87 E2
nson Court	87 F3	Dunolly Place	87 F4	Kinnessburn	87 E3	Priestden Park	87 F4
an Place	86 B5	East Scores	87 F2	Cottages (2)		Priestden Place	87 F4
ny Park	87 G3	Eddie Court	87 E3	Kinnessburn	87 E3	Priestden Road	87 F4
ny Place	87 E2	Ellice Place	87 E2	Gardens (1)		Priory Gardens	86 C4
Paterson Lane	86 A4	Fairway House (2)	86 A4	Kinnessburn Road	87 E3	Provost Niven Close	86 D3
ndra Court	87 E2	Fergusson Place	86 A3	Kinnessburn	87 E3	Queen's Gardens	87 E2
ndra Place	87 E2	Fife Park	86 B3	Terrace (3)		Queen's Terrace	87 E3
d Place	87 E2	Findlay Douglas	86 C5	Kirk Hill	87 F2	Radernie Place	86 A5
n Place	87 F3	Court		Kirkaldy Court	87 E4	Reid Gardens	86 B5
Robertson	87 E5	Fleming Place	87 E3	Kyle Gardens	86 A3	Rose Lane	87 E2
e		Forbes Place	86 A3	Ladebraes Lane	87 E2	Rose Park	86 D2
ew Lang	86 A4	Fordyce Court	86 D4	Ladebraes Walk	86 D3	Roundhill Road	87 F4
scent		Forgan Place	87 E4	Ladebraes Walk	87 E3	Ruthven Place	86 C4
ew Thom Place	87 G4	Forrest Street	87 E4	Lamberton Place	86 D5	St Gregorys (5)	87 F2
uther Road	87 G4	Fraser Avenue	87 E5	Lamond Drive	87 E4	St Leonards Fields	87 F3
e Court	86 D2	Freddie Tait Street	87 E4	Langlands Road	87 F3	St Leonard's Road	86 C3
e Street	86 D2	Gibson Place	86 D1	Largo Road	86 D5	St Mary Street	87 G3
Place		Gilchrist Row	86 C4	Lawhead Road East	86 B3	St Mary's Place	87 E2
erlonie Court	87 E4	Gillespie Terrace	87 E1	Lawhead Road West	86 B3	St Mary's Quadrant	87 E2
Burn Park	87 E3	Gillespie Wynd	87 E2	Lawmill Gardens	86 A4	St Nicholas Street	87 F3
Burn Road	87 E3	Glebe Road	87 F3	Lawpark	86 B4	Sandy Herd Court	87 E4
r Lane	87 F2	Golf Place	87 E2	Learmonth Place	86 C4	Sandyhill Court	87 E3
ur Place	87 G3	Gourlay Wynd	86 D4	Leonard Gardens	86 B5	Sandyhill Crescent	87 E3
carron Avenue	86 B4	Grange Road	87 G4	Letham Place	86 A4	Sandyhill Road	87 E4
month Court	86 D5	Grannie Clark's	86 D1	Lindsay Gardens	86 C4	Scooniehill Road	86 D5
Street	87 E2	Wynd		Links Crescent	86 D2	Scores, The	87 E1
Place	86 A4	Greenside Court	87 F3	Links, The	86 D1	Shields Avenue	87 F4
e Avenue	87 F3	Greenside Place	87 F3	Little Carron Gardens	86 A4	Shoolbraids	87 E4
y Jones Place	86 C5	Gregory Lane (4)	87 F2	Livingstone Crescent	87 E3	Shore, The	87 G3
ard Road	86 A4	Gregory Place	87 F2	Livingstone Place	87 E3	Shorehead	87 G2
Crescent	87 G4	Greyfriars Gardens	87 E2	Lockhart Place	87 E2	Sloan Street	86 D3
ster Place	87 G4	Guardbridge Road	86 C1	Logie's Lane	87 E2	South Castle Street	87 F2
e Street	87 E3	Guthrie Place	87 E2	Loudens Close	87 E3	South Street	87 E2
nfaulds Avenue	86 D4	Hallowhill	86 B4	Lumsden Crescent	86 A3	Southfield	87 E3
Embankment	86 D1	Hamilton Avenue	87 E4	McKenzie Square (1)	86 A4	Spinkie Crescent	86 C5
Street	87 E4	Hay Fleming	86 A4	Marine Place	87 F2	Spottiswoode	86 D4
anan Gardens	86 B3	Avenue		Market Street	87 E2	Gardens	
Wynd	87 E2	Hepburn Gardens	86 B4, D3	Mavis Haugh	86 C4	Station Road	86 D2
hill Gardens	86 B5	Hope Street	87 E2	Maynard Road	86 C4	Steading, The	87 G4
sden Gardens	86 C5	Horseleys Park	86 D4	Melbourne Place	87 E3	Straiton Wynd	87 E4
ngate	86 C4	Howard Place	87 E2	Mercat Wynd	87 E2	Strathkinness High	86 A3
Crescent	86 A4	Huntly Place	86 C4	Middleshade Road	86 C3	Road	
n Place	86 A4	Hutchison Court	87 E4	Moir Crescent	86 B5	Strathkinness Low	86 A3
berlain Street	87 E4	Irvine Crescent	87 F4	Montgomery Court	86 B4	Road	
bers Place	86 A4	Jacob's Ladder	86 D2	Morton Crescent	86 A4	Thistle Lane	87 E2
h Square	87 E2	James Foulis Court	86 C5	Muir Gardens	86 A3	Tom Morris Drive	87 E4
h Street	87 E2	James Robb Avenue	87 E4	Murray Park	87 E2	Tom Stewart Lane	86 D4

Trinity Place	86 B4	Beehives, The	96 B7	Hillpark Road	96 B6	Scotscraig	
Tulloch Place	86 B5	Birkhill Avenue	96 B6	Hillpark Terrace	96 B6	Scotswood Crescent	
Union Street	87 F2	Blyth Court	97 G3	Hillside Place	97 G3	Scott Street	
Viaduct Walk	86 D3	Blyth Street	97 G3	James Street	97 G2	Seacraig Court	
Walker Place	86 A3	Boat Brae	97 F3	Kerr Street	97 G2	Shepherd's Road	
Wallace Avenue	86 D3	Boat Road	97 F3	Kilgask Street	97 G2	Station Brae	
Wallace Street	87 E3	Braeside Road	97 E4	Kilmany Road	96 B7	Station Path	
Wardlaw Gardens	86 D2	Bridge Street	97 F4	Kilnburn	97 G3	Strathblair Avenue	
Warrack Street	87 F4	Bridge View	96 C5	Kinbrae Court	97 F4	Struan Place	
Watson Avenue	87 E3	Bridgehead Place	96 B6	Kinbrae Park	97 F3	Struan Street	
West Acres	86 A3	Castle Bank	97 E4	Gardens		Sylvan Lane	
West Burn Lane	87 F2	Castle Brae	97 E4	Kinbrae Park	97 F4	Tay Street	
West Port	87 E2	Craighead	97 H2	King Street	97 G2	Tay Terrace	
West Port Court	87 E2	Crescent		Kirk Road	97 F4	Tayfield Avenue	
West Sands Road	86 D1	Craighead Road	97 G2	Linden Avenue	97 G3	Tayport Road	
Westburn Court	87 F2	Craigshannoch	96 A6	Mars Gardens	96 D5	Tayview Terrace	
Westview	87 E3	Road		Marsh Lane	96 C5	Union Street	
Whitehill Terrace	87 E3	Crosshill Terrace	96 C6	Maryton	97 G2	Victoria Street	
Windmill Road	86 D2	Cupar Road	97 G3	Mount Stewart Road	96 B6	Viewmount Road	
Windsor Gardens	86 B5	Cuthbert's Brae	97 E4	Myrtle Terrace	97 G3	Waterston Crook	
Winram Place	86 C5	Cuthbert's Road	97 E4	Naughton Road	96 B6	Wellgate Street	
Wishart Gardens	87 E5	Devonlea Road	96 A6	Netherlea Place	97 E4	Wellpark Terrace	
Woodburn Place	87 G3	East Queen Street	97 G2	North Terrace	96 C5	East (2)	
Woodburn Terrace	87 G4	East Station Place	97 G2	Northfield Road	97 H2	Wellpark Terrace	
Younger Gardens	86 A4	Elizabeth Crescent	97 H2	Northview Terrace	96 B6	West (1)	
		Ericht Road	96 D5	Norwood	97 G2	West Acres Drive	
		Flass Road	96 D5	Norwood Lane	97 G2	West Park Road	

Index to Wormit & Newport-on-Tay

		Forgan Street	97 F4	Prospect Terrace	97 G2	West Road	
		Forgan Way	97 F4	Queen Street	97 G2	Westfield Terrace	
		Garland Place	97 F4	Rankine Court	96 D5	Westwater Place	
Albert Crescent	97 G3	Glenleven Drive	96 A6	Reservoir Road	96 B6	Westwood Terrace	
Alma Terrace	97 E4	Gowrie Street	97 G3	Riverside Gardens	96 C5	Whinfield Place	
Bank Street	97 G2	Granary Lane	97 F3	Riverside Lane	97 E4	William Street	
Bay Road	96 A6	Grenada Brae	97 G1	Riverside Road	96 C5	Woodbine Terrace	
Beach Road	96 C5	High Road	97 F3	Robert Street	97 G2	Woodhaven Avenue	
Beechwood Terrace East	97 F4	High Street	97 G3	St Fort Place	96 D5	Woodhaven Terrace	
		Highfield Avenue	96 C5	St Fort Road	96 D5	Woodmuir Crescent	
Beechwood Terrace West	97 F4	Hill Crescent	96 B6	St Mary's Lane	97 G3	Woodmuir Terrace	
		Hill Street	97 E4	St Phillan's Lane (1)	97 G3	Youngsdale Place	

3 Frazer Street, Largs, KA30 9HP
Tel: 01475 689242
Fax: 01475 675500
e-mail: sales@nicolsonmaps.com
website: www.nicolsonmaps.com

Ordnance Survey®
Mapping and Data Centre